MISSIONAL
Essentials

**A GUIDE FOR
EXPERIENCING
GOD'S MISSION
IN YOUR LIFE**

▶▶▶ **BRAD BRISCO** & **LANCE FORD**

the HOUSE studio

CONTENTS

ISBN 978-0-8341-5112-3

The House Studio
PO Box 419527
Kansas City, MO 64141

Copyright 2012 by Brad Brisco and Lance Ford

Cover Design: Arthur Cherry
Interior Design: Sharon Page

PART THREE: EXPERIENCING THE ESSENTIAL PRACTICES

www.thehousestudio.com   10 9 8 7 6 5 4

CULTIVATING MISSIONAL LIVING

HE WILL BUILD HIS CHURCH

Around the same time the Woodstock stage echoed Bob Dylan's prose, "The times, they are a changin'," a new breed of leaders mounted the podiums at ministerial conferences across North America. These were the "church growth" experts, who agreed with the legendary folk icon. Their response was to offer marketing ideas and techniques to the pastors and leaders of the rapidly declining churches throughout the United States.

For a while the new way of "doing church" appeared successful. The next twenty-five years or so would produce the largest Protestant churches in the history of the United States. Even church buildings began to change as customer service became a ministry mantra throughout church leadership circles. From indoor playgrounds that would make Chuck E. Cheese turn green with envy to cozy cafes and comfy sermons, the response to "felt needs" was offered on a weekly basis to churchgoers everywhere as leaders engineered services aimed at "seekers" and began to view church members as clients. Pastors and church staffs worked tirelessly to draw people into the confines of the church campus.

Now, looking back at over four decades of church growth strategies, Christianity in North America is further down the road of decline than before the experts began their vastly influential endeavors. In fact, many sociologists predict the wholesale collapse of a significantly measurable Christianity over the next century.

All of that sounds like pretty dire news. Thankfully, there is, as the late Paul Harvey would say, "The rest of the story." Over the past few years, thousands of Christian leaders have begun to humbly reexamine the message and ways of Jesus and are rediscovering his commandment, "Go, and make disciples," and his declaration, "I will build my church."

Missional Essentials is about that very thing. It is written to help Christ followers rediscover the heart of God for our neighborhoods and communities. He invites us on a journey of *going as* the church rather than just *coming to* the church.

HOW DO WE DEFINE "MISSIONAL?"

The word "missional" is simply the adjective form of the noun "missionary." It is used to describe people and churches who operate as missionaries in their local contexts. In a more comprehensive, classic definition of missionary, it describes a church that sees God's mission as the organizing principle that defines, shapes, and *sends* the church to participate in what God is already doing in the world.

WHO IS THIS GUIDE WRITTEN FOR?

- *Everyday Christians* who are searching to follow Jesus and live their faith in the real world and who have a desire to better understand and practice what it means to live with mission in the normal routines of their daily lives.
- *Church and ministry leaders* who are looking to engage more deeply the practical ways and means of missional living and who need help leading their congregations in a faithful missional journey.

WHAT ARE THE IDEAL CONTEXTS FOR USING THIS GUIDE?

- *Existing Leadership Teams* that have begun to investigate the missional conversation and are interested in studying the concepts and practices together.
- *Small Groups* that are interested in exploring the paradigms and biblical directives toward missional community.
- *Church Planting Core Teams* that are seeking to develop a DNA of missional principles and practices as a way of shaping and forming their faith communities.

HOW TO VIEW THIS LEARNING JOURNEY

Missional Essentials is a response to Jesus' commandment for us to love God with our all in all: "He answered, 'Love the Lord your God with all your heart and with all your soul and with all your strength and with all your mind'; and, 'Love your neighbor as yourself'" (Luke 10:27). Each lesson includes components that engage our heart and soul, mind, and strength, as we move forward on the missional quest of loving our neighbors as ourselves.

Being—Heart and Soul

Spiritual formation is a lifelong journey of expanding our capacity to live from the heart of Jesus. For a spiritual life to be formed, we need discipline, practice, and accountability. By engaging in the habits of spiritual formation, our ministry emerges naturally from the depths of our *being*— who we are—rather than from the sweat of *doing*. Scripture reading and meditation, prayer, and reflective reading are some of the key components that synchronize for inner transformation.

Knowing—Mind

Growing in understanding and knowledge through studying Scripture and other writings is essential for equipping ourselves missionally. The information you will study with others is presented through a variety of definitions, readings, and Scripture readings within each lesson.

Doing—Strength

Information alone will not bring about change. We need experiences that move us to *doing* the skills and practices we have just learned. In order to skillfully master a subject, apprentices must have the opportunity for hands-on application. Practicing and living out the principles of a particular subject are essential for true transformation.

Reflecting

Each lesson begins with a time of sharing the results from the previous week's "doing" assignment. The collective voice of the group will yield both insight and encouragement, as well as celebration of what God is doing in the lives of everyone involved.

HOW ARE THE LESSONS STRUCTURED?

Missional Essentials is designed in a one lesson per week format over a twelve-week period. Each lesson is structured to take approximately an hour and a half, depending on your learning style and your desire to dig deeper with the suggested study resources. In addition to the handbook materials, there is also a weekly Missional Action that is created to enhance the learning experience of each lesson. Each weekly lesson is organized around the following six elements:

Previous Lesson Reflection

The first few minutes of each week's lesson include a time of looking back on the missional engagement from the previous week's lesson. It is important to have time to listen and learn from others who are making the missional quest.

Central Theme

The central theme serves as the key idea around which the lesson is built. In addition to a basic definition, there are a couple questions that help introduce the idea. The remainder of the lesson is designed to bring clarity and further understanding of the central theme.

Biblical Reflection

Missional engagement must be rooted in the example and teaching of Jesus. Therefore, each lesson includes a biblical study and reflection to orient us toward the person and message of Jesus.

Reading

Each lesson includes a reading that is intended to bring additional insight to the weekly discussion. The reading combines the best missional thinking from a collection of authors as well as practical advice for missional living from practitioners in a variety of settings.

Reading Reflection

All readings conclude with reflection questions to help reinforce essential principles and further the learning experience.

Missional Action

Each lesson concludes with one or more actions to assist in moving us from missional principles to real world practices. The missional actions will not only accelerate the learning curve but will provide practical opportunities to begin participating in God's mission.

LESSON

1

HIS NATURE
*Our
Missionary
God*

IN THIS LESSON

Central Theme: The Missionary Nature of God and His Church

Biblical Reflection: Isaiah 6:1-8; Isaiah 61:1-2; Luke 4:18-19; John 20:21

Reading: Capturing a Missionary Vision

Reading Reflection: Being Sent

Missional Action: Seeing and Responding to God's Missional Work

The Missionary Nature of God and His Church

The word *mission* is from the Latin *missio,* which means "sending." It is *the* central biblical theme describing God's activity throughout history to restore and heal creation. Mission is not primarily an activity of the church, but an attribute of God. He is a sending, missionary God who sends a missionary church.

1. What comes to mind when you think of the attributes of God?

2. What do you think about "mission" being *the* central biblical theme of the Bible? How might this change the way you view Scripture?

Isaiah 6:1-8; Isaiah 61:1-2; Luke 4:18-19; John 20:21

1. *Read Isaiah 6:1-8.* What do you learn about God from Isaiah 6? What is significant about Isaiah's response to God's question in this passage? In what ways is God still asking this question today?

2. *Read Isaiah 61:1-2 and Luke 4:18-19.* What specifically did Isaiah say he was sent to do? Reflect on each deed mentioned. Do you think the actions listed in Isaiah 61 could serve as a picture of the gospel? What is the significance of Jesus making an application of the Isaiah passage to his own ministry?

3. How has God called and sent you as a missionary to participate in his mission? How do the actions listed in Isaiah 61 relate to your life and ministry? Do you sense a "sending" call to participate in any of the activities mentioned?

4. *Read John 20:21.* Who is the sender in this passage? Who is Jesus sending in this passage? What do you think they are sent to do?

5. What questions do these passages raise for you?

Capturing a Missionary Vision

When you hear the word "missionary," what is the first thought that comes to mind? A person going overseas? A foreign country? Maybe Africa? If you were to look up the word "missionary" in the dictionary, you would read something like this: "a person undertaking or sent on a mission." Well, that isn't very helpful. Don't you hate it when a dictionary uses a form of a word to define the word you are looking up? What about that word "mission?" If you were to look up the word "mission" in the dictionary you would read something like, "the act of sending or being sent."

Initially, this definition may not seem to be overly helpful, either, but it is actually quite insightful. The idea of mission can relate to either *sending* or *being sent*. The problem with this definition is that in the church, we have focused almost exclusively on the idea of *sending* rather than *being sent*.

We think primarily of sending and supporting missionaries in faraway places rather than seeing ourselves, both individually and collectively, as being sent. This reality leads us to the first theological essential that must undergird all of our missional activity—the understanding that God by his very nature is a missionary God, and we as the church, are his missionary people.

The Missionary Nature of God

Mission is the grand narrative of Scripture. The entire Bible is generated by and all about God's mission. The word "mission" is from the Latin *missio*, meaning "sending." It is *the* central biblical theme describing God's activity throughout history to restore and heal creation. While often overlooked, Scripture is full of sending language that speaks to the missionary nature of God.

From God's sending of Abram in Genesis 12 to the sending of his angel in Revelation 22, there are literally hundreds of examples of God as a sending God. Perhaps the most dramatic illustration of sending in the Old Testament is found in Isaiah 6. In this passage, we catch a glimpse of God's sending nature, "Then I heard the voice of the Lord saying, 'Whom shall I *send*, and who will go for *us*?'" To this Isaiah responds, "'Here am I! *Send* me!'" (6:8).

Later in the book of Isaiah there is a fascinating passage where the prophet recognizes that God's Spirit has anointed him to "proclaim good news to the poor" and *sent* him to "bind up the brokenhearted" (61:1). In the larger passage of Isaiah 61:1-3 it is interesting to note that there are no fewer than six redemptive deeds that proceed from or are dependent on the verb "sent" or the phrase "he has sent me." To emphasize the centrality of the sending theme, the passage could be rendered this way:

He has *sent* me, to bind up the brokenhearted;

He has *sent* me, to proclaim freedom for the captives;

He has *sent* me, to release from darkness the prisoners;

He has *sent* me, to proclaim the year of the Lord's favor and the day of vengeance of our God;

He has *sent* me, to comfort all who mourn, and provide for those who grieve in Zion;

He has *sent* me, to bestow on them a crown of beauty instead of ashes, the oil of gladness instead of mourning, and a garment of praise instead of a spirit of despair. (61:1-3, paraphrased).

If this passage is familiar it may be because Jesus applies it to his own ministry in Luke 4:18-19 as he claims to be the fleshly embodiment of Isaiah 61:1-2. It becomes, in a sense, the closest thing to a personal mission statement for Jesus.[1]

When moving to the New Testament, sending language is found throughout the Gospels, the book of Acts, and each of the Epistles. However, the most comprehensive collection of sending language is found in the Gospel of John, where the words "send" or "sent" are used almost sixty times. The majority of uses refer to the title of God as "one who sends" and of Jesus as the "one who is sent."

In the final climactic sending passage in John's Gospel, Jesus makes clear that he is not only sent by the Father, but now he is the sender, "'As the Father has *sent* me, I am *sending* you'" (John 20:21).

With this statement, Jesus is doing much more than drawing a vague parallel between his mission and ours.[2] Deliberately and precisely he is making his mission the model for ours, saying, "'As the Father has sent me, I am sending you.'" Therefore, our understanding of the church's mission must flow from our understanding of Jesus' mission.

The Missionary Nature of the Church

The purpose of the previous, very brief survey of sending language is not merely to emphasize the missionary nature of God, but to highlight the importance of understanding the church as a *sent*, missionary entity. God is a missionary God who *sends* a missionary church. That is why the word "missional," when properly applied, is helpful. The word is simply the adjective form of the noun "missionary." It is used to describe the church as those who operate as missionaries in their local contexts. At the core of the missional conversation is the idea that a "genuine missional impulse is a *sending* rather than an *attractional* one."[3] In other words, we should be sending people in the church out among people of the world rather than attempting to attract people of the world in among the people of the church. This is a helpful distinction because most people do not think of the church in sending, missionary terms.

In the book *The Church Between Gospel and Culture*, theologian George Hunsberger offers three different ways people view the nature of the church.[4] The first view is what Hunsberger calls the "Reformation Heritage." He says that Protestants have inherited a particular view of church that emphasizes the right preaching of the Word, the right administration of the ordinances, and the proper exercise of church discipline. This view, he argues, has left us with an understanding of the church as "a place where certain things happen." Therefore, the church is defined primarily as a *place* a person goes to hear the Bible taught, to participate in the Lord's Supper and baptism, and, in some cases, to experience church discipline.

Hunsberger calls the second view "Contemporary Variation." He believes that while the church in North America is not far removed from viewing church as "a place where certain things happen," a more accurate description of the way many people view the church today would be as "a vendor of religious goods and services." From this perspective, members are viewed more as customers for whom the religious goods and services are produced. Churchgoers expect the church to provide a wide range of religious services such as great worship music, children's programs, small groups, parenting seminars, and so on.

One of the major problems with both of these first two views is that the church is seen as an institution that exists for the benefit of its members.

The third view of the nature of the church is identified as the "Missionary Vision," or what Hunsberger more often refers to as a body of people *sent* on a mission. Central to this view is understanding the chuch as a people *called and sent* by God to participate in his mission for the world. The church still gathers together, but the difference is that we don't gather for our own sake, but instead for the sake of others, or better yet, for the sake of God's mission. We come together as a collective body of believers to be equipped through prayer, worship, and study in order to be *sent* out into the world. The church is to be a gathered *and* scattered people.

> The church is the bearer to all the nations of a gospel that announces the kingdom, the reign, and the sovereignty of God. . . . It is not meant to call men and women out of the world into a safe religious enclave but to call them out *in order to send them back as agents of God's kingship.*[5]

Why This All Matters

To drive home the importance of understanding the church as a collection of missionaries, or "sent agents," consider the concept of cultural distance,[6] a tool designed to assess how far a person or people group is from a meaningful engagement with the gospel. Look at the following scale:

$$m0 \qquad m1 \qquad m2 \qquad m3 \qquad m4$$
$$l{-}{-}{-}{-}{-}{-}l{-}{-}{-}{-}{-}{-}l{-}{-}{-}{-}{-}{-}l{-}{-}{-}{-}{-}{-}l$$

Each numeral with the prefix *m* indicates a significant cultural barrier to the meaningful communication of the gospel.[7] Barriers include such things as language, race, history, worldview, traditions, beliefs, political affiliation, and so on.

In *The Forgotten Ways*, author Alan Hirsch offers a description of how each section of the scale might look in a local church context, assuming that the church "stands" at the m0 on the above scale:

m0–m1 Those with some concept of Christianity who also speak the same language, have similar interests, most likely share the same nationality, and are from a similar class grouping as you or your church. Most of your friends would probably fit into this bracket.

m1–m2 Here we would include the average non-Christian in our context: A person who has little real awareness of, or interest in, Christianity and is somewhat suspicious of the church. This category might also include those previously offended by a bad experience with church or Christians. Just go to the average local pub/bar or nightclub to encounter these people.

m2–m3   People in this group have absolutely no idea about Christianity. Or they might be part of some fringy subculture or an ethnic group with different religious impulses. This category might also include people marginalized by Christianity – e.g. the gay community. But m2–m3ers are also likely to be described as people actively antagonistic toward Christianity as they understand it.

m3–m4   This group might be inhabited by ethnic and religious groupings with a bad history of the church – e.g., Muslims or Jews. The fact that they are in the West might reduce some of the distance, but just about everything else gets in the way of a meaningful dialogue. They are highly resistant to the gospel.[8]

The reason this discussion is important for the missional conversation is because the church in the U.S. operates *almost exclusively* in the sphere of m0–m1, as shown in the following illustration.

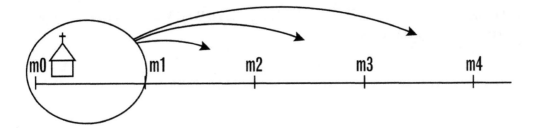

The attractional approach to church is *generally* effective at connecting with those in the m0–m1 realm. However, there are two very significant problems with this approach. First, the population in the U.S. is increasingly defined by the descriptions of those in the m1 to m4 categories. More and more people find themselves further away from the influence of the church.

Second, the attractional posture of most churches requires those outside the reach of the church to do the crosscultural work to find Jesus. In other words, we are asking those who are far away from God to become like missionaries and cross over the cultural barriers to come to us. But it is the church that comprises the missionary people of God. *We are the ones who are sent!*

Being Sent

1. How would you describe the difference between *sending* and *being sent*?

2. What thoughts do you have about the missionary nature of God?

3. Do you find Hunsberger's three views of the church helpful? Why? Which of the views best describes your perspective of the church?

4. What thoughts do you have on the church being both called *and* sent, or gathered *and* scattered?

5. What thoughts do you have on the concept of cultural distance? How does this help you understand the importance of the missionary nature of the church?

6. How does this lesson influence the way you think about your own life?

7. What questions do you have about this lesson? How does this lesson challenge or convict you?

Seeing and Responding to God's Missional Work

1. Identify at least two people groups or geographical locations in your city or neighborhood to which God is looking to "send" someone.

2. List areas in your life that may need to change for you to be able to say "Here am I. Send me!" What is the first step you will take to overcome each hindrance?

How might you respond to these same questions from the perspective of your church?

1. Identify at least two people groups or geographical locations in your city to which God is looking to "send" your church.

2. List areas in the life of your church that may need to change for the church to be able to say "Here are we. Send us!" What is the first step your church might take to overcome each hindrance?

LESSON
2

HIS WAY
*Incarnational
Ministry*

IN THIS LESSON

Reflection on Lesson 1: His Nature

Central Theme: The Incarnation and the Church's Ministry

Biblical Reflection: John 1:1-18; Philippians 2:1-11; John 20:21

Reading: As the Father Has Sent

Reading Reflection: Missional and Incarnational

Missional Action: Seeing and Responding to God's Missional Work

LESSON 1: *His Nature*

1. Briefly share how you responded to the Missional Action from last week's lesson. What people groups or locations did you identify?

2. What areas of your life did you identify need changing for you to be sent by God? What obstacles or concerns are still hindering you from making changes?

3. What other reflections have you had on Lesson 1?

4. What reflections do you have on the other stories that were told in your group?

The Incarnation and the Church's Ministry

The word *incarnation* literally means "in the flesh." It refers to the act of God entering into the created world as the man Jesus of Nazareth. Although the word is not found in the Bible, it is based upon the opening words of John's Gospel: "In the beginning was the Word, and the Word was with God, and the Word was God" . . . "The Word became flesh and made his dwelling among us" (1:1, 14). The phrase *incarnational ministry* speaks to the reality that the Word became flesh in Jesus; it also commends the church as the body of Christ to be "enfleshed" in every culture and present with those to whom God has sent us.

1. How might Jesus "dwelling among us" speak to the way we do ministry?

2. What would it look like for you to dwell with those to whom God has called you?

John 1:1-18; Philippians 2:1-11; John 20:21

1. *Read John 1:1-18.* What does it mean to you when you read in verse 14, "The Word became flesh and made his dwelling among us"?

2. In *The Message* paraphrase John 1:14 reads, "The Word became flesh and blood, and moved into the neighborhood." What thoughts come to mind when you think of Jesus moving into your neighborhood? What does this teach us about God's way of identifying with us?

3. *Read Philippians 2:1-11.* What does this passage add to the idea of Jesus dwelling among us? What does it mean to "value others above yourselves"? How might Jesus' example of emptying himself serve as a picture for ministry?

4. *Read John 20:21.* Focus on the first portion of this verse. If the second half of the verse speaks to the fact that Jesus sends his disciples, what is the main point of the first portion of the passage?

5. What questions do these passages raise for you?

As the Father Has Sent

The first lesson examined the missionary nature of God and the "sentness" of the church. God is a missionary God who *sends* a missionary church. We learned that "missional" is an adjective to describe the church as a sent, missionary entity. However, this is only half the story. Alan Hirsch speaks of the "missional-incarnational impulse," where the word *missional* expresses the sending nature of the church, while *incarnational* represents the embedding of the gospel into a local context. In other words, "missional" speaks to our direction—we are *sent*, while being "incarnational" is more about *how* we go, and *what* we do as we go.

The Incarnation

The word *incarnation* comes from a Latin word that literally means "in the flesh." It refers to the act of incredible love and humility whereby God took it upon himself to enter into the depths of our world so that the reconciliation between God and humanity may be brought about.[9] The Incarnation is God's ultimate missional participation in creation (John 3:16-17). When God entered into our world in and through the person of Jesus, he came to live among us. "The Word became flesh and blood, and moved into the neighborhood" (John 1:14a, TM).

Incarnational Living

"The Incarnation not only qualifies God's acts in the world, but must also qualify ours. If God's central way of reaching the world was to incarnate himself in Jesus, then our way of reaching the world should likewise be incarnational."[10] However, not everyone believes that the Incarnation should serve as a model for mission. Some believe that the phrase "incarnational ministry" is misleading or even dangerous. During a doctoral seminar, I [Brad] had a seminary professor who took great exception to the use of the word "incarnational" when describing a certain mode of ministry. He believed that the Incarnation was a unique historical and theological event that could not be emulated, and therefore, should not be connected in any way to human activity.

There is absolutely no doubt that the Incarnation of Jesus was a special, unrepeatable event. Further, as we enter into the world of others, we certainly cannot take on another's identity in the fully integrated way that Jesus did. But *surely* we can make a distinction between *the* Incarnation with a capital "I" and incarnational ministry.

Obviously there is nothing wrong with inviting believers to model their lives after the life of Jesus. The apostles encouraged Christians to imitate Christ as a way of identifying with him. Both Peter and Paul insisted that Jesus is to be the model for Christian living.

> "To this you were called, because Christ suffered for you, leaving you an example, that you should follow in his steps" (1 Peter 2:21).

> "Follow my example, as I follow the example of Christ" (1 Corinthians 11:1).

Peter makes clear that Jesus' life is to be our example. And Paul states simply that we can follow his way of life because he is so closely following the way of Jesus. Missiologist Michael Frost elaborates on the theme of following Christ's example from the book of Philippians:

> Paul makes this point even more strongly in Philippians, in which he tells us that our "attitude should be the same as that of Christ Jesus" (Philippians 2:5). We often assume that this passage then commends to us Jesus' humility, which is clearly present in the text. But Jesus' humility is commended to us insofar as it is expressed in his commitments to *identification* and *relinquishment*. First, to follow Jesus' example means that we should share his profoundly humble identification with sinful humankind (Philippians 2:7b-8a). Second, those of us who wish to emulate Jesus should be aware of his equally humble willingness to empty himself and make himself nothing for the sake of God's redemptive purposes (Philippians 2:6-7a). . . . To embrace an incarnational ministry, then, involves a willingness to relinquish our own desires and interests in the service of others.[11]

Frost's examination of the Philippians passage speaks of two very important ideas related to incarnational ministry—the concepts of "proximity" and "presence."

Incarnational ministry must involve living in close proximity with others. "We cannot demonstrate Christlikeness at a distance from those whom we feel called to serve."[12] Just as Jesus took on flesh and blood and moved into the neighborhood, we must do likewise. This may require moving geographically to be closer to those to whom God has sent us. At the very least it will demand creating time and space to be directly and actively involved in the lives of people we are seeking to reach.

The concept of presence moves beyond mere proximity to identification and surrender. Jesus identified *with* and advocated *for* those he was called to. As the Philippians passage makes clear, he humbled himself. He literally emptied himself for the sake of others. This realization suggests an incarnational approach that calls us to relational identification with our neighbors that will lead to tangible acts of love and sacrifice.

It is helpful to recognize that Jesus' words from John 20:21, "'As the Father has sent me, I am sending you,'" are most often used to emphasize the sending of the disciples, and subsequently the church. But we must not neglect the first half of the passage. Jesus says, "'As the Father has sent me.'" The word translated *as* (or in some translations *just as*) means "like" or "in a similar manner." In other words, we need to be sent *like* Jesus was sent. To whom, and in what manner was Jesus sent? He was sent to the down and outers of society. He was *with* and *for* tax collectors, the oppressed, the poor, and the diseased. Again, taking Jesus as our example, we are called to do likewise.

In an excellent book titled *The Incarnation and the Church's Witness*, theologian Darrell Guder provides a very helpful summary on the incarnation of Jesus and its relationship to what it means to be a Christian:

> We arrive at the concept of incarnational witness as one way of expounding on the character of our missionary vocation. In the incarnation of Jesus Christ, God revealed himself as the One who is *with and for* his creation. Now, as the Risen Lord sends his Spirit to empower the church, we are called to become God's people present in the world, *with and for* the world, like St. John pointing always to Christ. The most incarnational dimension of our witness is defined by the cross itself, as we experience with Jesus that bearing his cross transforms our suffering into witness.
>
> Incarnational witness is, therefore, a way of describing Christian vocation in terms of Jesus Christ as the messenger, the message, and the model for all who follow after him. To speak of the incarnation missionally is to link who Jesus was, what Jesus did, and how he did it, in one great event that defines all that it means to be Christian.[13]

Nuts and Bolts

So what does all this talk of identification, proximity, and presence have to do with daily living? It may sound like a cliché, but it really is all about relationships. It's about getting close enough to people to listen, understand their hopes and dreams, and actually come to like and love them as individuals.

The Gospels tell us that Jesus was a friend of sinners. Hear that—a friend. What constitutes a friend? When another person invites you to meet *their* friends. The Bible is full of examples of people inviting Jesus to meet and spend time with their friends. There was a sense of whimsical holiness about Jesus that drew people to him. Someone once said that people who were not *like* Jesus, *liked* Jesus. As followers of Jesus, shouldn't that also be true of us? That doesn't happen without living with and among people. So what will it take for you to incarnate the life of Jesus in your community? What will it take for you to really move into your neighborhood, perhaps for the very first time?

Missional and Incarnational

1. In your own words how would you describe the "missional-incarnational" impulse?

2. How do you understand *the* Incarnation informing, or setting an example for, incarnational ministry?

3. Do you believe there are some legitimate concerns for using incarnational language to describe an approach to ministry? If so, what are they?

4. How would you describe the concept of proximity? What about the concept of presence?

5. How does this lesson influence the way you think about where you live and how you live?

6. What questions do you have about this lesson? What aspects of this lesson challenged or convicted you? Why?

Seeing and Responding to God's Missional Work

1. Ask yourself, *Am I in close proximity to those to whom God has called me? What will I do this week to encourage proximity?* Identify one way to experience greater proximity and act upon it.

2. Ask yourself, *Am I experiencing incarnational "presence" with those I live near? Do I identify and understand the fears and concerns of those around me?* Now determine one way to experience a greater level of presence and act upon it.

LESSON 3

JOINING HIS PURPOSES

Participating in the Missio Dei

IN THIS LESSON

Reflection on Lesson 2: His Way

Central Theme: God's Mission Has a Church

Biblical Reflection: John 3:16-17; 5:24; 14:26; 16:7; 17:18; 20:21

Reading: Mission vs. Missions

Reading Reflection: The Church and God's Mission

Missional Action: Seeing and Responding to God's Missional Work

---

REFLECTION ON

LESSON 2: His Way

1. Briefly share how you lived out the Missional Action from last week's lesson. How did it change or influence the way you understand the concept of living incarnationally?

2. What did you do to encourage proximity in your neighborhood? What did you learn?

3. What did you do to encourage a sense of presence with those near you? What did you learn?

4. What did you learn about yourself? What might you do differently next time?

5. What reflections do you have on the other stories that were told in your group?

God's Mission Has a Church

CENTRAL THEME

The phrase *missio Dei* is Latin for "the sending of God." In English it is often rendered as "the mission of God." *Missio Dei* language emphasizes that mission is not primarily an activity of the church, but rather the activity of God. The church is God's instrument sent into the world to participate in his mission. Therefore, the church exists because of God's mission, not the other way around.

1. What thoughts do you have about the church existing because of God's mission instead of the church *having* a mission?

2. How might the concept of *missio Dei* change the way you think about the church?

John 3:16; 5:24; 14:26; 16:7; 17:18; 20:21

The classic understanding of the *missio Dei* involves three movements: God the Father sending the Son; God the Father and the Son sending the Spirit; God the Father, Son, and Spirit sending the church into the world.

1. *Read John 3:16-17; 5:24.* What do you learn about the sending nature of God and his mission from these verses? What questions do these verses raise?

2. *Read John 14:26; 16:7.* What difference do you notice between these two verses? In what ways do you think the Spirit empowers God's mission?

3. *Read John 17:18; 20:21.* Describe the setting for these two passages.

Mission vs. Missions

READING

The third key element in missional theology is the concept of *missio Dei*. An English rendering of this Latin phrase speaks to the "mission of God." It is God who has a mission to set things right in a broken, sinful world—to redeem and restore it to what he has always intended.

Therefore, mission is not the invention, responsibility, or program of the church. Instead it flows directly from the character and purposes of a missionary God. In the words of South African missiologist David Bosch, "It is not the church which undertakes mission; it is the *missio Dei* which constitutes the church." Or stated in a slightly different way, "It is not so much that God has a mission for his church in the world, but that God has a church for his mission in the world."[14]

It is not only crucial to understand that God has a mission, it is equally important to understand that his mission is larger than the church. We in the church often wrongly assume that the primary activity of God is in the church, rather than recognizing that God's primary activity is in the world, and the church is God's instrument sent into the world to participate in his redemptive mission. Instead of thinking of the church as an entity that simply *sends* missionaries, we should instead view the church *as* the missionary. Among other things, this shift in perspective will bring about radical changes in two particular areas.

First, a *missio Dei* perspective will shape our thinking about the form and function of the church. Typically, congregations view missions as simply one program or activity among many other equally important functions of the church. Therefore, the missions *program* is seen alongside those programs such as worship, small groups, men's and women's ministries, youth and children's ministry, and so on. When missions is viewed in this way, the main business of many mission committees "is to determine how to spend the mission budget rather than to view the entire congregational budget as an exercise in mission."[15] However, when the church begins to define itself as an agent of God's mission, it will begin to organize every activity of the church around the *missio Dei*.

> Mission as the organizing principle means that mission goes way beyond being some sort of optional activity or program for our churches. It actually is the organizing axis of the church. The life of the church revolves around it. This is not to say that we don't do corporate worship, develop community, and make disciples, but that these are catalyzed by and organized around the mission function. Only in this way can we be truly missional. Merely adding serving events or special outreach days to our church schedules will not develop missional people nor make a missional church.[16]

To ensure clarity on this issue of God's mission as the organizing principle for all other activities of the church, let us state again that this does not minimize the need and importance of the other functions of the church. It is simply stating that no other function of the church can rightly be the organizing principle, or the reason we come together in the first place. Worship should not be the organizing principle. Community should not be the organizing principle. Even discipleship and evangelism should not be the organizing principles.

Instead, worship, community, discipleship, evangelism, and every other important activity of the church are properly understood and initiated only when viewed through the lens of mission. The images below provide an illustration for the move from "missions" as one among many functions of the church to "mission" being *the* organizing principle for all other activities or ministries of the church.[17]

MISSIONS	ARTS	CHILDREN	SMALL GROUPS	YOUTH	TEACHING	WORSHIP

MISSION

ARTS	CHILDREN	SMALL GROUPS	YOUTH	ET C.	TEACHING	WORSHIP

The second significant shift that occurs with a *missio Dei* perspective deals with our starting point for mission activity. When we begin to see the church (individually and collectively) as the sent, missionary people of God, we no longer view the church as the jumping-off point when thinking about mission. Rather, we look for God's activity in our local setting as the place to begin our missional engagement.

Among other things, this means the nature and shape of mission cannot be decided beforehand, but must be discerned in relation to God's participation in a local context. Instead of front-loading mission plans and strategies with what we think the people in a community need, we begin by listening and learning what God is already doing. Only after discerning what God is doing in a particular setting do we then ask how God wants us to participate with him. Another way to frame this conversation is to consider the four D's of missional engagement.

Discover

If it is truly God's mission and not ours, then we must discover where God is at work. The first step in discovering what God is doing is through listening. Individually and collectively we must cultivate our ability to listen well on three fronts—we must listen to God, the local community, and each other. It is simply impossible to ascertain the movement of God without carving out significant time to listen to his voice through prayer and Scripture as well as the voices of those we desire to serve.

Discern

In addition to listening, participating in God's mission will involve the difficult task of discernment. Not only will we need to discern what God is already doing, but we will need to ask the follow-up question, *In light of my (our) gifts and resources, how does God want me to participate in what he is doing?* The fact is we can't do it all, which is true for both individual followers of Jesus as well as local congregations. But it is also true that God has gifted us all to do something! The point of discernment is to determine where and how to participate in God's mission.

Do

This may seem obvious, but the process of discernment is useless if we do not obey what God is calling us to do. When God prompts us to participate in what he is doing in the lives of others, we must be obedient to respond.

A story told by one of our friends, Sam, illustrates these first three points. Sam purchased a house in a very impoverished part of town. His intentions were to create a mission house that would be home to several volunteers as they invested in the life of the neighborhood for the purpose of seeing community transformation take place. One of their first projects was the adoption of the local elementary school. The plan was to invest in the school by providing tutoring to students, serving the teachers, and providing simple maintenance for the school facilities. Who could argue with these great ideas?

One day Sam decided to share his vision for the school with Nacho, a man who lived just across the street. He had two children who attended the school, and surely he would be very pleased to learn of Sam's plans. However, as Sam began to share with him what they were gearing up to do, Nacho asked Sam to walk outside to the sidewalk in front of the house. At that point, Nacho pointed up above their heads to the streetlight. He said to Sam, "If you really want to be a blessing to this neighborhood, then get that streetlight back on." At first Sam was a little bewildered. It was in the middle of the afternoon on a hot summer day. *What's so important about a streetlight?* Sam thought. Nacho began to tell Sam that when the streetlight was not on it wasn't safe for the kids to play outside after dark. When the streetlight wasn't on, drug deals would go down on the corner. When the streetlight wasn't on, cars got broken into.

Nacho then told Sam that he had been trying to get the city to come out and fix that light for nearly a year. Sam called the city authorities, and that afternoon the streetlight was back on. There was apparently a language barrier that was prohibiting Nacho from making the proper city department connection.

After I [Brad] heard that story, I told Sam that he should refer to it as the "ITSS" story. It's The Streetlight, Stupid! The point is that no matter how great our plans for a community might be, it may not be what the community really needs. We can't assume we know. Instead, we must listen—listen to God and listen to the community. Then we must act.

Debrief

Throughout the process of engaging God's mission we must create opportunities to reflect on our missional involvement. Sometimes this may simply mean we need individual down time to reflect upon our activities. We may need to ask God to affirm our involvement, or to ask for clarity of direction. But it will also mean we must carve out time to reflect with others in our faith community. We need to hear what others are seeing and sensing concerning God's activities and to hear the stories of how others are engaging God's mission. In this way it is important for us to be in the position to offer feedback.

To participate in the *missio Dei* is to play a personal and vital role in the movement of God's redemptive mission. God is inviting us into his missionary adventure.

The Church and God's Mission

1.   What thoughts do you have as you reflect on the David Bosch quote: "It is not the church which undertakes mission; it is the *missio Dei* which constitutes the church"? What about the follow-up quote, "It is not so much that God has a mission for his church in the world, but that God has a church for his mission in the world"?

2.   How would you describe the difference between the church *sending* missionaries versus the church *being* the missionary?

3.   What would it look like for your group or church to be "God's instrument *sent* into the world"?

4.   How might the various ministries in your church look if mission were the organizing principle? What about youth ministry? Small groups? Children's ministry? Worship ministry?

5.   In what ways are the "4 D's" helpful? Can you give examples of how you or your church has front-loaded missions? How could you and your church do a better job in the area of discernment?

Seeing and Responding to God's Missional Work

Throughout the week, identify at least three situations in which you ask the following questions:

    1.   Where do I see God at work? Where and how is God working in the lives of those around me? Where and how is God working in my neighborhood? What about my place of vocation?

2. In light of my gifts and resources, how does God want me to partner with him in what he is doing?

How might you respond to these same questions from the perspective of your church?

1. In light of your church's gifts and resources, how might God be calling your church to participate in the *missio Dei*?

2. What specific and unique gifts and resources has God given your local church?

LESSON

4

TURNING HIS WAY

Living a Kingdom of God Agenda

IN THIS LESSON

Reflection on Lesson 3: Joining His Purposes

Central Theme: A Different Way of Living

Biblical Reflection: Matthew 6:25-33; Matthew 3:1-2; Matthew 4:17

Reading: Recalculating: Entering the Kingdom

Reading Reflection: His Will Be Done

Missional Action: Seeing and Responding to God's Missional Work

LESSON 3: *Joining His Purposes*

1. Briefly share how you lived out the Missional Action from last week's lesson. How did it change or influence the way you thought as you went through your regular routines this week?

2. How did you see God at work in the midst of the Missional Action? What did you learn about where and how God is working?

3. What did you learn about your gifts and resources? Where and how do you think you are supposed to partner with God?

4. What reflections do you have on the other stories that were told in your group?

A Different Way of Living

Jesus invites us to live our lives very differently from the non-Christ-following world around us. Some people have called this the upside-down nature of the kingdom of God, and it is within this kind of counterintuitive nature that Jesus so often spoke. He told us that if we want to be first we must be last. If we want to be greatest we must choose to be least. These concepts look great on Bible pages but become very difficult to actualize in the realities that make up our own day-to-day living.

1. Share your initial thoughts about the upside-down nature of the kingdom of God. Practically speaking, how might "first being last" play out in our day-to-day lives?

2. How would you best describe or define entering the kingdom of God?

Matthew 6:25-33; Matthew 3:1-2; Matthew 4:17

1. *Read Mathew 6:25-33.* How does your level of anxiety coincide with what Jesus says in this passage? In what areas of life are you currently anxious?

2. How might your life change if you were to seek first the kingdom of God?

3. *Read Matthew 3:1-2.* Consider the phrase "the kingdom of heaven is at hand." What does it mean for something to be *at hand*?

4. *Read Matthew 4:17.* From these passages we observe that both John the Baptist and Jesus proclaimed, "'Repent, for the kingdom of heaven has come near.'" What does this mean for you at this point in your life?

Recalculating: Entering the Kingdom

READING

From time to time, we find ourselves driving along a highway or boulevard only to realize we have either missed a turn or have been going in the wrong direction for quite some distance. Maybe we were talking on the phone, lost in a song from the radio, or caught up in pointless mind wandering. Whatever the reason, we discover we are going the wrong way. Perhaps we notice a road sign that alerts us to our misdirection, or the voice from our GPS instructs us to "Turn around when possible," followed by the phrase, "Recalculating." You may be surprised to know that the voice would be accurate if it began by shouting, "Repent!" which means, "turn around."

Repent. It comes across as a rather stern, austere word—one that is not commonly used in today's vernacular. One of the only times we hear or see it is on a bumper sticker warning us to turn from sin or face the fires of hell, or from a street preacher warning of impending doom upon all of mankind. But as we look at the Gospels, we see that of all the words they could have used, both John the Baptist and Jesus chose the word *repent* as the first commandment regarding the arrival of the kingdom of God. Both men issued a stark warning to the entire region of Galilee that its citizens were going in the wrong direction and that they needed to turn around immediately.

The kingdom of God is not something we build or establish. It is a realm—God's realm of rule—that we enter into, that we receive. Just about every area of the kingdom of God that we want, or should want, to enter into requires us to repent, to turn around. What is it that we are turning from? And what are we turning toward? Primarily, we are turning around from our own ways and means of command and control. We are turning around from our own demands to have our own way and to accumulate all that we can for our own selfish stockpile. We are turning to God and saying, *You are in control of my life. Your supply is sufficient for me. Lord, if you want me promoted, or noticed, you can make it happen.* If we want to experience the realm of God's peace, we must become peacemakers. If we want to inherit the earth, we don't fight for it. We learn meekness (Matthew 5:5). If we want to live in the realm of God's mercy, we become merciful ourselves.

In pointed contrast to the kingdoms of men, which are established and sustained through accumulating more and more via coercion and power, Jesus' kingdom is authenticated and perpetuated by the authority of love. The Jesus kind of love lays down its rights and privileges every day. This is what it means to pick up our cross *daily.*

Love is not merely a stepping back or a pacifistic stance. It does not stop at, "Don't return evil for evil." Rather, it moves forward, proactively. It says, "Return good for evil." The silver rule is "Do not do unto others what you do not want them to do to you." The golden rule—Jesus' rule—is "Do unto others what you would have them do unto you." So Jesus tells his Jewish listeners that when a Roman soldier acts upon his legal (but oppressively and morally gross) right to have them carry his gear for one mile, to smile and "carry it two miles."

The ongoing effect of the kingdom of God is that it constantly brings a holy disruption to our lives. It messes with our plans and definitions of both what is needed in life as well as who is worthy of our attention and devotion. This is the essence of servanthood in the kingdom of God.

In our case, we have signed our lives over to Jesus as Lord and Master. The glorious irony of it all is that rather than going into bondage, we move into the deepest essence of freedom we could have ever imagined. We are free from the never-ending loop of always trying to get ahead. Scholar Johannes Metz says,

> It is not a liberation from our powerlessness, but from our own form of predominance. It frees us, not from the state of being dominated but from that of dominating; not from our sufferings but from our apathy; not from our guilt but from our innocence, or rather from that delusion of innocence which the life of domination has long since spread out through our souls.[18]

We do not have to read far into the Gospels to see that Jesus clearly expects his followers to remain fully active within all aspects of culture but to do so from a different set of values and motivations. Henri Nouwen says,

> It is important for us to realize that Jesus in no way wants us to leave our many-faceted world. Rather, he wants us to live in it, but firmly rooted in the center of all things. Jesus does not speak about a change of activities, a change in contacts, or even a change of pace. He speaks about a change of heart. This change of heart makes everything different, even while everything appears to remain the same. This is the meaning of "Set your hearts on his kingdom first . . . and all these other things will be given you as well." What counts is where our hearts are.[19]

It is the redemptive nature of the kingdom of God that shapes our values and motives. God wants us to possess and exercise power, but power from him, not fleshly power. The account of Satan's temptations of Jesus in the wilderness (Matthew 4:1-11) paints a vibrant picture of the motives and means of Jesus and the kingdom of God in contrast to the motives and means of the kingdom of darkness. Satan tempts Jesus in three ways:

FOOD—*that which sustains life itself*

The deceiver attempts to bring the focus upon us as the only trusted provider for our livelihood. Jesus models the posture of the follower of God. It is the word of God that is the overarching sustainer of life. By feeding on and obeying the Word, we will be fulfilled and sustained in all aspects of life.

SAFETY AND SECURITY—*who and what controls our life*

Fear and anxiety are at the top of the list of tactics the minions from the kingdom of darkness use to control us. Jesus was firm in his faith, radically trusting the Heavenly Father. He looked to God as the one who was in charge of his life and destiny.

GLORY—*our source of meaning*

Satan offered Jesus the kingdoms of the world if he would only fall down and worship him. That offer is still on the table for us all. The truth about worship is that what or who we worship shapes our identity. Some people worship fashion, or cars, or living in a certain style or size of home. They want to be identified with a certain brand or status. The obsession becomes idolatrous. True worship of God means that we derive our identity from him.

The wilderness temptations that Jesus overcame provide us with an idea of what to expect on a consistent basis during the power encounters between the two opposing kingdoms. Craig Van Gelder explains,

> The children of the kingdom also live by a different set of values. They are guided by a different set of expectations. And they live out of a different source of power. This event confirms the character of the kingdom of God. Those who would follow Jesus must realize they are entering into a cosmic conflict with the enemy, a conflict they can win only by the power of the Spirit.[20]

Undoubtedly, most of us fail to maintain a conscious awareness of the spiritual battle we are in as children of the Light. The kingdom of darkness is as real as the chair you are sitting in right now. It is unrelenting. Drawing our strength from the Lord is not only our only hope for victory; it is a *sure* hope for victory. Happily, the only fight we have is the fight of faith. The rest of the battle is up to God. Living a lifestyle whereby we seek God's agenda first and foremost is the initial and ongoing step toward the missional journey. If we are serious about entering the kingdom of God here and now, we agree to God's terms and God's turns. As Nouwen said, "What counts is where our hearts are."

His Will Be Done

READING REFLECTION

1. Before reading this week's lesson what was your concept of what it means to repent? What did it involve and what did it lead to?

2. What is your reaction to the Johannes Metz quote regarding being freed from our own dominating? Look back over the quote and share your reaction.

3. In what ways have the three areas of temptation—food, safety and security, and glory—as discussed in the reading, held power in your life?

4. How mindful have you been of the "fight of faith" that is constantly being waged as Satan seeks to tempt you with same temptations he tried on Jesus?

5. What might it look like for your group or church to move proactively into the kingdom of heaven in your particular community or locale?

Seeing and Responding to God's Missional Work

Throughout the week, do your best to keep the following questions in mind:

1. What areas do I need to concentrate my repentance upon in order to lay hold of the kingdom of God?

2. How can I assume the posture of a servant today? How can I serve in the situation at hand?

At the end of each day this week, reflect over your day and ask:

1. In what ways do I believe Satan has tempted me with sustenance, safety and security, and finding my source of meaning through status?

2. Today did I do unto others the way I would have them do unto me? How so?

LESSON
5

HEAR O' CHURCH

*One Lord,
One Life*

IN THIS LESSON

Reflection on Lesson 4: Turning His Way

Central Theme: Committing Our Whole Lives to God

Biblical Reflection: Deuteronomy 6:1-9; Mark 12:29-31; Romans 12:1-2

Reading: Lord Over All

Reading Reflection: Living the Confession

Missional Action: Seeing and Responding to God's Missional Work

LESSON 4: *Turning His Way*

1. Briefly share how you lived out the Missional Action from last week's lesson. How did it change or influence you as you went through your regular routine this past week?

2. How did you see God at work in the midst of the Missional Action? What did you learn about where and how God is working?

3. What did you learn about yourself? What might you do differently next time?

4. What reflections do you have on the other stories that were told in your group?

Committing Our Whole Lives to God

Living in the twenty-first century presents a unique set of challenges for those of us in the developed world. Modern conveniences and technology certainly make chores and routine tasks easier, but they also coincide with a lifestyle of disconnectedness from others around us. For the most part, our lives are compartmentalized in such a way that we live with a lack of integration. We speak of our work life, recreational life, family life, and spiritual life. The result for many of us is a *disintegrated* life.

1. Think about the people in your life across the different spheres of your routines—home, work, play, church, shopping, and so on. How integrated is your life?

2. What does the phrase, "The Lord your God is *one* Lord" mean for you?

3. Share your thoughts on the concepts of sacred places and secular places.

Deuteronomy 6:1-9; Mark 12:29-31; Romans 12:1-2

1. *Read Deuteronomy 6:1-9 and Mark 12:29-31.* As you reflect upon this passage, in what ways have you faithfully loved God with all of your heart, all of your soul, and with all of your strength? In what ways have you held back?

2. Who are the people in the spheres of your life from whom you have withheld your "whole heart, soul, and strength"?

3. What idols in your life are hindering you from loving God and loving others with your whole life?

4. *Read Romans 12:1-2.* If worship means offering our whole lives back to God, how might that bring change in your current living? How can you offer your life back to God on a daily basis? Read *The Message* version of Romans 12:1-2 and reflect from this perspective.

READING

Lord Over All

Ours is a culture totally different from the audience that sat at Jesus' feet. His listeners were not comprised of twenty-first century Westerners who are mostly a reasoning and scientifically-minded society. The ancient Near East people were deeply spiritual and consciously aware of sacred, mystical, and even magical realms. Theirs was a culture that was filled with a number of gods and demigods. They were pluralists. Virtually every sphere of life had a god that was seen as ruling over it. There was the god of the forest, the god of family, the god of the river, the god of the harvest, and so on. Each and every god was feared and had to be negotiated with and appeased on a regular basis.

It was within this culture that one of the local scribes approached Jesus to ask him what the most important commandment was (Mark 12:29-31). Imagine that. Out of all the commandments in the Old Testament, this guy wanted Jesus to narrow them down to the top *one*. How could this be possible? After all, Yahweh himself issued each and every commandment. They were all important. Every single precept came from the lips of God. How could one commandment stand above the rest?

Throughout the Gospels when Jesus was asked a question, he answered it with another question, or even a parable. This was a typical rabbinic method of teaching. However, on this occasion, departing from his normal way of responding, Jesus not only answered the question posed to him; he did so quickly and plainly.

It would not have been unreasonable to expect Jesus to respond, as he so typically did, by asking another thought provoking question. It is easy to imagine Jesus saying, *Look around at the fields and mountains; see the lake teeming with fish and all manner of creatures. Which of all these that God has created is most important?* Christ could have said, *Every commandment is God breathed and not one is more or less important than the other.* But Jesus immediately answered straight away and without hesitation. And he went further; he gave the guy a two-for-one deal: Jesus told the scribe the number one most important commandment *plus* the number two most important commandment.

> "The most important one," answered Jesus, "is this: 'Hear, O Israel: The Lord our God, the Lord is one. Love the Lord your God with all your heart and with all your soul and with all your mind and with all your strength.' The second is this: 'Love your neighbor as yourself.' There is no commandment greater than these." (Mark 12:29-31)

Listen Up

The commandment Jesus proclaims as the most important is known as the *Shema*, which means "hear." What we are to *hear* is that there are not a multitude of gods (polytheism). The implication is that one God is Lord over every part of our lives, bar none. Nothing lies beyond his claims or power. This idea obliterates the concept of sacred and secular places in our lives (dualism). Our God is God from bedroom to boardroom, from workplace to play place, from living room to schoolroom, and every place in between. Missiologists Michael Frost and Alan Hirsch succinctly comment on the *Shema*:

> Deuteronomy 6:4 is the claim of Yahweh over against the competing claim of the many other gods in the polytheistic religious environment of the day. It is a call for the loyalty of the people. This statement is therefore an attack on heathen religious polytheism rather than just a statement about so-called "ethical monotheism" of the later speculative theologians. The claim has direct and concrete implications: It is a call for the Israelites to live their lives under the Lordship of one God and not under the tyranny of the many gods. In other words, it is a practical call not to live one's life as if there were a different god for every sphere of life—a god of the field, a god of the river, a god of fertility, a god of the sun, and so forth.

> Judaism loudly proclaims that there is only one God and he is Lord of every aspect of life. Again, here the concrete and practical nature of Hebraic thinking comes to the fore. Polytheists can compartmentalize life and distribute it among many powers. But as Maurice Friedman rightly says, "The man in the Israelite world who has faith is not distinguished from the 'heathen' by a mere spiritual view of the Godhead, but by the exclusiveness of his relationship to God, and by his reference of all things to him." Monotheists (really, biblical believers) have only one reference point. This is the biblical mode of thinking—concrete and practical, as opposed to theoretical and speculative. The implications are far reaching, not as simple theology, but as practical missiology. A re-Hebraizing of Christianity is so vital for the emergence of the missional-incarnational church.

> This claim to unify our lives under the one God (called *yichud* by the rabbis) has truly radical implications for us today as we struggle to find new ground on which to base our

discipleship. Biblical monotheism means that we cannot live like there is one "god" for the church and another for politics and another in economic life or still another for the home. No, all of life, every aspect of it, every dimension, is to be brought under and unified under the *one* God, Yahweh. Seen in this light, the *Shema* is a claim of God's exclusivity and a direct challenge from God about the role of idols in the believer's life. In the first, and original, instance it has nothing to do with the Eternal Being of God.[21]

Especially in a culture such as ours, where a lack of integration in every sphere of our lives is the norm, the importance of understanding and acting on the truth of the *Shema* cannot be overstated. Our society is one that lacks connection between the people and the places that make up our lifestyle patterns. The people we work with are not the same people we see in our favorite coffee shop. The folks that we see at the gym are not the same ones we see at the mega grocery store. And none of these people are members of our own local church.

There are only one or two types of places most people, Christian and non-Christian alike, consider to be sacred. These spots are official places of worship—church, synagogue, and mosque—and home. The remaining places we call secular territory. If you ask most Christians, they consider their places of work, recreation, education, commerce, and marketplace to all be secular spaces.

Lord of All

Secular, by definition, means "non-sacred" or "apart from God." Theologians call this idea *dualism*, a terribly dangerous precept that not only limits God, but limits mission. The subconscious result of the dualistic divisions means that most Christians compartmentalize spirituality into the two sacred boxes of church and home. Therefore, we consider the people we encounter in differing territories the same way. Especially in evangelical circles, the people that occupy "non-sacred" spaces often become categorized as *them* within the *us vs. them* delusion that has become part of the sacred-secular divide.

With the *Shema*, Jesus is saying that all dimensions of our lives are under his care, joy, and rule. God gets out of the stained glass box of church and moves into every sphere of society. We—those filled with his spirit—can (and should) begin to understand all of life as ministry and worship. This idea is echoed in the legendary movie, *Chariots of Fire*, in which Eric Liddell says, "I believe God made me for a purpose, but he also made me fast. And when I run I feel his pleasure."

So as we seek to *Shema* (to hear) we aim to recognize God's activity throughout our daily routines. By understanding that God is everywhere and seeking to restore and redeem broken people and the brokenness throughout all of creation, our lives take on new meaning—spiritual meaning. Henri Nouwen says,

> There is a real tendency to think of the spiritual life as a life that will begin when we have certain feelings, think certain thoughts, or gain certain insights. The problem, however, is not how to make the spiritual life happen, but to see where it actually is happening. We work on the premise that God acts in this world and in the lives of individuals and communities. God is doing something right now. The chipping away and sculpting is taking place whether we are aware of it or not. Our task is to recognize that, indeed, it is God who is acting, and we are involved already in the spiritual life.[22]

The sacred-secular divide as a mindset, or paradigm, has enormous implications for the life of the Christian. When we live under this misguided belief, we leave God out of the equation of the majority of our actual daily living. But when we seek to hear God in our daily routines, believing that the Lord is bringing his kingdom to earth, we hear and see things we might have never observed beforehand.

For Christian businessmen and women this means that the phrase, "This is business" is no longer an acceptable excuse for shady dealings, or even lopsided deals where we aim to get everything we can even if it means driving the other person out of business because, after all, *this is not spiritual; this is just business.* Understanding *Shema* means we understand that God is just as much in on this deal as he is in on Sunday morning praise and worship.

Understanding God is one Lord over all things and beings keeps us tuned in to—hearing—his voice in every situation. He is Lord of café, gym, workplace, bus ride, fast food restaurant, neighborhood . . . everything, every place. The apostle Paul said, "For from him and through him and for him are all things" (Romans 11:36). In the very next verse he continues,

> So here's what I want you to do, God helping you: Take your everyday, ordinary life—your sleeping, eating, going-to-work, and walking-around life—and place it before God as an offering. Embracing what God does for you is the best thing you can do for him. Don't become so well-adjusted to your culture that you fit into it without even thinking. Instead, fix your attention on God. You'll be changed from the inside out. Readily recognize what he wants from you, and quickly respond to it. (Romans 12:1-2, TM)[23]

On the basis of the fact that God is over all and in all situations, Paul appeals to us to offer our whole world up to God in worship. He is Lord over every dimension of life. Since God is *One* we have the obligation to "bring every aspect of our lives, communal and individual, under this One God, Yahweh."[24]

The *Shema* is one of the most practical and catalytic passages in all of Scripture. It is no wonder that Jesus calls it the most important commandment of all. It calls us to bring our minds, hearts, and bodies under the complete lordship of Jesus. God is no longer understood as involved in just the "spiritual" dimensions of our lives, because we have eliminated the sacred-secular divide from our concept of God and life in general.

This is a cornerstone precept of the biblical worldview. We commit our whole life to God. Nothing is off limits. If the entire world, including our immediate world, and all that is within it is truly under the ownership of God, then there can be no part of my life that is not open to his rule.

It is very possible to be a confessing *monotheist* (belief in one God), while being a practicing *polytheist* (belief in multiple gods). To confess Jesus is Lord means our loyalty is with him throughout every sphere of our lives, including our sexuality, activity as consumers, roles as neighbors, workers, and friends. We have one life, under one Lord.

Living the Confession

1. Before reading this week's lesson, how much thought had you given concerning the differing compartments of your life?

2. Up to this point in your journey, in what ways have you viewed the world from the perspective of a sacred/secular divide?

3. What has been your basic concept of worship before this lesson? In what ways has this session re-formed your thinking about worship?

4. Think about your own life for a moment. Consider the people and events that form your normal rhythm of living. Where do you carry out the actual living of your life? Who are the people that you frequently interact with, and where are the places you most often can be found? Think about these places:

   - Grocery store
   - Gym or golf course
   - School
   - Coffee shop
   - Church
   - Workplace
   - Bank
   - Auto shop
   - Salon or barbershop

5. In *The Message* translation of Romans 12:1-2, Eugene Peterson writes, "Take your everyday, ordinary life—your sleeping, eating, going-to-work, and walking-around life—and place it before God as an offering." Discuss how this might change the way you approach your day-to-day life.

PART TWO
EXPERIENCING THE
ESSENTIAL PRINCIPLES

Seeing and Responding to God's Missional Work

1. This week, decide how you can demonstrate/practice your love for the Lord with your heart (inner passion), your soul (mind), and your strength (body). Give yourself a daily assignment for each area, such as prayer (heart), reading (mind), and serving someone (strength).

2. Based on Romans 12:1-2, what "sacrifice" of worship will you offer up to God this week?

3. Take some time to meditate on the *Shema*, asking the Lord how you can most faithfully love God and neighbor.

4. What was your experience today in practicing your love for the Lord in the three spheres of heart, soul, and strength?

LESSON

6

THE PAST IS NOW

Living in a Mission Field

REFLECTION ON

LESSON 5: *Hear O' Church*

1. Briefly share how you responded to the Missional Action from last week's lesson. How did you live out the Shema this past week?

2. What was your "sacrifice" of worship to God this past week?

3. What other reflections have you had on Lesson Five?

4. What reflections do you have on the other stories that were told in your group

The Rise and Fall of Christendom

Christendom is the term given to describe the religious culture that has dominated Western society since the fourth century, when the Roman Emperor Constantine made Christianity the official religion of the Roman Empire. Post-Christendom refers to the time *after* Christendom, when the church lost its place of power and influence. The rise and fall of Christendom has created a unique set of issues for the church today.

1. What examples come to mind when you consider the influence of Christianity on American culture?

2. What examples might illustrate the diminishing influence of Christianity on American culture today?

Jeremiah 29:1-9 (Exiles in a Foreign Land)

When thinking about the decline of Christendom from a biblical perspective, many people turn to the metaphor of exile. It is popular to think about the post-Christendom church living as exiles, similar to the nation of Israel when taken into Babylonian captivity in 586 BC. There are certainly parallels between the contemporary Christian experience of displacement, uncertainly, and irrelevance, and the struggles of the Jews in Babylon.[25] However, this may not be the best metaphor. The idea of exile presupposes a desire to be restored to a previous way of life. The exiled Jews hoped for a time when their lost kingdom would be reestablished. When applied to the church in a post-Christendom era, it may lead some to place their hope in the return of Christendom. This is *not* what the church, or the world for that matter, needs today.

Instead, the church would be better served by looking at the words of Jeremiah, the prophet who spoke during the time of the Babylonian exile. Jeremiah challenged the Jews who had been taken into exile to withstand the desire to return to a restored Israel. He urged them to accept their new situation as the will of God and to seek God's blessing for those they perceived as their enemies. Jeremiah called on them to seek the welfare of the city where God had sent them into exile (Jeremiah 29:7).

While the church today may feel a sense of exile, brought to a place of uncertainly and unfamiliarity, let us not desire to return to a time of Christendom. God is not calling us to return to things of old, but to participate in something completely new.

1. What do you think of when you hear the word "exile"? What do you think about its use as a metaphor for the church today?

2. How do the words of Jeremiah change the way you think about being exiled?

3. What questions do these passages raise for you?

We're Not in Kansas Anymore

Remember the famous line from the 1939 film *Wizard of Oz*, when Dorothy first arrives in Oz and realizes she is now in a world that is strangely different? "Toto," she says to her little dog, "I've a feeling we're not in Kansas anymore." Dorothy's surroundings were now unfamiliar. The people and places she was used to seeing no longer existed. She had no idea where she was, but one thing was certain—everything around her had drastically changed.

A place that is strangely different describes the setting for the church today. The world has seemingly changed so quickly and radically that many churches feel like exiles in a foreign land. Like Dorothy, many churches no longer recognize their surroundings. They don't completely understand the changes that have taken place; they only know that things are not like they used to be.

Christendom to Post-Christendom

There are numerous factors that have influenced the change we see today in Western culture. Issues such as globalization, urbanization, post-modernism, and the rise of the information age have all had significant influence on the church. However, nothing has shaken the foundations of the church over the centuries as much as the rise and fall of Christendom.

In 313 AD, the Roman Emperor Constantine adopted the Christian faith as his own and decided to replace paganism with Christianity as the official imperial religion. "He invited the church to come in from the margins of society, where it had been operating for the previous three centuries, and join him in Christianizing the empire."[26] Giving great resources and favors to the church, Constantine set in motion a process that would eventually bring all of Europe into a church-state relationship known as Christendom.[27] It is difficult to overstate the impact Constantine's decision had on the Christian faith. A few of the changes that took place included:

- The assumption that all citizens were Christian by birth
- Infant baptism as the symbol of necessary incorporation into the Christian society
- Sunday as the required day of church attendance, with penalties for noncompliance
- The definition of "orthodoxy" as the common belief shared by all, which was determined by powerful church leaders supported by the state
- The construction of massive and ornate church buildings
- A strong distinction between clergy and laity, and the relegation of the laity to a largely passive role
- The increased wealth of the church and the obligation of required tithes to fund the system
- The division of the globe into either "Christendom" or "heathendom" and the waging of war in the name of Christ and the church
- The use of political and military force to impose the Christian faith[28]

The net effect of Christendom over the centuries is that Christianity "moved from being a dynamic, revolutionary, social, and spiritual movement to being a static religious institution"[29] with its corresponding structures, priesthood, and rituals. The Christian faith moved from being an integrated way of life that was lived out seven days a week to being an obligation that was fulfilled by attending a service at a set time.

By the middle of the twentieth century, however, it was becoming clear in Europe that Christendom was in serious decline. People began to use the term "post-Christendom" to describe the church's loss of social privilege. Others used it to refer to Western civilizations that no longer considered themselves to be Christian.

In this era of post-Christendom, the church once again returned to the margins of society. It had lost its position of prominence and control. While once the majority, in post-Christendom the church was in the minority. The shift from marginalization to control, and then back again is illustrated in the following diagram.[30]

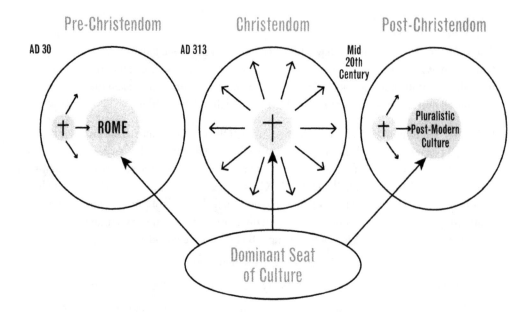

PART TWO
EXPERIENCING THE
ESSENTIAL PRINCIPLES

The image shows that before Constantine the dominant influence in society was the Roman Empire and the church was a marginalized sect, located on the outskirts. However, the church was making serious inroads into the empire. During the time of Christendom, the church became the dominant seat of culture, albeit corrupted with political and military power. Today, the picture is of a church that has been relegated back to the margins. Author Reggie McNeal refers to this time of transition as "30 [AD] all over again."

However, it is important to note that while those outside the church understood that Christendom was fading, many inside the church struggled to realize the church was losing its footing. Consequently, much of the church was at a loss as to how to reach into the changing pluralistic, postmodern culture that had little interest in the church.

What Difference Does It Make?

Here is the important point in this whole discussion: the difficulty the church is experiencing today of relating to the current culture is in large part due to our Christendom heritage. Many in the church today still believe that Christianity is in a place of influence and significance. Many still operate under the false assumption that Christendom is alive and well. While there may be *some* parts of the country that still cling to Christian values, the vast majority of the population is rapidly moving away from the things associated with the church. In the eyes of many outside the church, the church has become completely irrelevant.

The decline of Christian influence in the United States can be seen in multiple ways. The most prominent example is the continual drop in church attendance. But it doesn't end with attendance. In fact, every indicator that can be used to measure church health reveals decline. Look at it any way you like. Conversions. Baptisms. Membership. Retention. Participation. Giving. Religious literacy. Effects on the culture. They are all in decline.[31]

This creates the setting for an enormous problem. At the same time that the church is less and less effective at reaching a changing world, many in the church continue to believe that the church maintains a central role in the life of culture. So instead of leaning toward the missionary vision of the church discussed in Lesson 1, we default to church as a "place where certain things happen" and we wrongly assume that those outside the church will be interested. But as we can see from all of the statistics, that simply isn't the case.

Going back to the *Wizard of Oz*, there is a scene later in the film where Dorothy reaches up to pick an apple from a tree, and the tree grabs the apple and slaps her hand. "Ouch!" Dorothy shouts. "What'd'ya think you're doing?" says the tree. "We've been walking a long way and I was hungry," replies Dorothy. The tree responds, "Well, how would you like to have someone come along and pick something off of you?" Dorothy answers, "Oh, dear! I keep forgetting I'm not in Kansas!"

Like Dorothy, we must not forget that the religious landscape around us has drastically changed. We are in a new land. At times we may feel like exiles in an unknown foreign land but, unlike many exiles, let us not yearn for what once was. Instead, let us seek to bring life and vitality to the land where God has placed us. Let us pray and toil for God's kingdom to come to the cities and neighborhoods in which we live.

It may be a hard pill to swallow for many, but the reality is the United States is *not* a Christian nation. And the sooner we can come to grips with that reality, the sooner we can return to the revolutionary, missional movement that is exemplified for us in the early church. We must see that it really is 30 AD all over again!

Understanding the Change

1. Of the list of changes that took place from Constantine's decision to make Christianity the official religion, which do you think were most damaging? Why?

2. In what ways do you see the lingering effects of Christendom today?

3. What examples illustrate for you that we now live in a post-Christendom culture?

4. In what ways does the diagram help you visualize the change that has taken place? Is there anything you would add to the image?

5. How might this lesson influence the way you live your life? How might it influence the life of your church as it interacts with the world?

6. What questions do you have about this lesson? What aspects of this lesson challenged or convicted you? Are there tensions you are experiencing with this lesson?

Seeing and Responding to God's Missional Work

Someone has said that until we fully grasp the fact that we live in a post-Christendom, post-Christian country, the church will be incapable of making the necessary changes.

1. This week, be mindful of examples you see that illustrate a post-Christendom culture. What do you hear in people's conversations? On television? In movies? In other media? List them here:

2. List the changes that you may need to make in your life in order to live as a missionary in a foreign, post-Christendom land. What steps will you take to incorporate the first change?

3. List the changes that your church may need to make in order to connect with those who are no longer interested in things of the church. What steps will you take to help the church incorporate the first change?

LESSON

7

RED LIGHT, GREEN LIGHT

Renewing and Refreshing for the Long Haul

IN THIS LESSON

Reflection on Lesson 6: The Past Is Now

Central Theme: Strengthened in the Lord

Biblical Reflection: Luke 24:49; Isaiah 40:31; Mark 2:27; Proverbs 4:23

Reading: Hitting the Pause Button

Reading Reflection: Developing Red Light, Green Light Habits

Missional Action: Seeing and Responding to God's Missional Work

LESSON 6: *The Past Is Now*

1. Briefly share how you lived out the Missional Action from last week's lesson, "Living in a Mission Field." How did noticing post-Christendom influence the way you think about the fabric of your own life?

2. How did you see God at work in the midst of the Missional Action? What examples did you see of a post-Christendom culture?

3. What other reflections do you have on Lesson 6? What reflections do you have on the other stories that were told in your group?

Strengthened in the Lord

American culture is the most medicated and therapeutic society on the face of the earth. Stress is killing us physically, emotionally, and spiritually. As God's people, it does not have to and should not be this way. If we will look to the Scriptures, we will discover a pattern for living—in any era—that God has prescribed to set his people free from stressful lifestyles. It is impossible for any of us to garner the strength to carry out life. The Lord never intended us to do so. He wants to be our strength for living.

1. Do you consider your life to be stressful?

2. Does the idea a stress-free lifestyle seem realistic? Explain why or why not.

Luke 24:49; Isaiah 40:31; Mark 2:27; Proverbs 4:23

1. *Read Luke 24:49.* What is significant about Jesus' instructions to the early disciples to wait in Jerusalem? In what ways is Jesus still instructing us to do this today?

2. *Read Isaiah 40:31.* What is the most difficult part of "waiting on the Lord" for you personally? Share some of the habits or spiritual disciplines you currently practice in order to renew your strength.

3. What has Sabbath meant to you up to this point in your life? In what ways do you observe or "keep" the Sabbath?

4. *Read Proverbs 4:23.* How do you personally "guard" or watch over your own heart life?

Hitting the Pause Button

Maybe you remember playing Red Light, Green Light as a child. The game is a combination of running and stopping, moving and freezing. To win, you must listen keenly to whoever is calling out the commands for stopping or going: "Red light! Green light!" In today's church, we are seeing a renewed obedience to Jesus' command to "Go, ye therefore." However, Jesus' last words when he appeared to the disciples after his resurrection were, "'Wait (stop) in the city until you have been clothed with power from on high'" (Luke 24:49)—"Red light!" So, in the midst of this study, as we focus on the much neglected "red light" aspects of missional living, it is imperative that we take time to focus on the habit of pausing, refreshing, and renewing ourselves in the Lord.

There is a tremendous amount of material available to sharpen us in Bible study, prayer, and other important spiritual disciplines. Those essential aspects of spiritual formation are not our focus in this study. This lesson is designed to sharpen our understanding and senses toward the necessity of stopping—waiting upon the Lord and renewing ourselves by his presence and by the beauty of his creation.

Listening in Solitude

Ours is a culture that values production to such a degree that the idea of "wasting time" for just about any reason is considered anathema. Henri Nouwen wrote, "The discipline of prayer is the intentional, concentrated, and regular effort to create space for God. Everything and everyone around us wants to fill up every bit of space in our lives and so make us not only occupied people, but preoccupied people as well."[32] This conditioned productivity affects our approach to prayer. Most of us have a tendency to approach prayer just as we would any other task to be completed. When we try to make our prayer time *useful*, we view it from a what-will-this-do-for-me perspective: What wisdom can I get? Will I feel God's presence? What answer will God give to my questions? Prayer becomes another daily chore. Nouwen writes,

> The world says, 'If you are not making good use of your time, you are useless.' Jesus says: 'Come spend some useless time with me.' If we can detach ourselves from the idea of the usefulness of prayer and the results of prayer, we become free to "waste" a precious hour with God in prayer. Gradually, we may find, our "useless" time will transform us, and everything around us will be different. Prayer is being unbusy with God instead of being busy with other things. To not be useful is to remind myself that if anything important or fruitful happens through prayer, it is God who achieves the result. So when I go into the day, I go with the conviction that God is the one who brings forth fruit in my work, and I

do not have to act as though I am in control of things. I have to work hard; I have to do my task; I have to offer my best. But I can let go of the illusion of control and be detached from the result. At the end of the day I can prayerfully say that if something good has happened, God be praised.[33]

As we set aside time for God to share his inward thoughts with us, we open our ears and the doors of our hearts to receive his most intimate affection and dreams for our lives and for those with whom we are in relationship and proximity. Isaiah 40:31 encourages us with, "Those who hope in the LORD will renew their strength."

Sabbath

For most Christians, especially those of us in the West, the concept of Sabbath is not only misunderstood, it is largely dismissed. It is most certainly rarely practiced and enjoyed. But correctly understood, the Sabbath simultaneously becomes a joy and a gift from God to us. It becomes a "get to" enjoy rather than a "have to" endure. One of the best hints of this perspective comes from Jesus himself as he responded to the heckling of the Pharisees. Jesus responded, "'The Sabbath was made for man, not man for the Sabbath'" (Mark 2:27).

Another clue for understanding Sabbath's intent is found by observing the children of Israel as they journeyed through the wilderness. The Lord supplied them with miracle food each day on the floor of the barren desert. However, the people still had to go out daily and collect the manna. God instructed them to gather only the day's needed supply of manna or it would become wormy. A few Israelites tested this and sure enough, the manna turned wormy and stank. So each day the task of gathering God's provision was undertaken. Every day, that is, except the seventh. God instructed that on the sixth day two days' supply was to be gathered and prepared. It would remain fresh on the seventh day. The Israelites were to rest on the Sabbath and enjoy God's provision. This was both a gift and a test for the people of God. Would they trust God to make a life for them? And would they accept God's gift of a refreshing, joy-filled day each week?

Missional community leader Sean Gladding says, "To take a day of rest is to resist the internal forces that drive us to assert ourselves through our activity. It is to refuse to conform to the restlessness of the culture we find ourselves in, to cease our tireless striving to reshape the world in our own image."[34] Though our bodies certainly need rest from daily toil, the Sabbath is given to us for far more than bodily replenishment. Rabbi Abraham Heschel writes:

> To the biblical mind . . . labor is the means toward an end, and the Sabbath as a day of rest, as a day of abstaining from toil, is not for the purpose of recovering one's lost strength and becoming fit for the forthcoming labor. The Sabbath is a day for the sake of life. Man is not a beast of burden, and the Sabbath is not for the purpose of enhancing the efficiency of his work. "Last in creation, first in intention," the Sabbath is "the end of creation of heaven and earth." The Sabbath is not for the sake of the weekdays; the weekdays are for the sake of Sabbath. It is not an interlude but the climax of living.[35]

Author Dan Allender says, "37% of Americans take fewer than seven days off per year. Only 14% take vacations of two weeks or longer. Americans take the shortest paid vacations in the world, and 20% of those who do take vacation days stay in touch with the office."[36] As un-American as it sounds, Sabbath observance means we schedule one day of *doing nothing* into our week. The first tenet of the Westminster Catechism reads, "The chief end of man is to glorify God and to enjoy him forever." *Forever* begins here and now.

God is more than capable of keeping the universe going without us helping out one day of the week. Sabbath should be a weekly event we look forward to with anticipation. What brings you joy? What gives you delight? If it is reading a book just for pleasure, then kick back and do it on your Sabbath. Whatever you do, don't work. Sabbath is not a day for you to get things done around the house. Remember, Sabbath is for joy and delight.

Daily Office

Author Pete Scazzero writes, "The word *Office* comes from the Latin word *opus*, or 'work.' For the early church, the Daily Office was always the 'work of God.' Nothing was to interfere with that priority."[37] The basic goal of the Daily Office is to maintain a conscious connection with the Lord throughout our day. St. Benedict structured eight prayer times, or *offices*, for monks. Every three hours the monks would stop whatever they were doing—including sleeping—and observe the office.

Few people other than monks observe eight offices today. Many people craft three or four offices, which are typically formulated around small doses of written prayers, reading a psalm, prewritten devotions, and scripture passages. There are several good books available to help us in observing the Daily Office, including *Common Prayer* by Shane Claiborne and *The Divine Hours* by Phyllis Tickle. You decide on the content of your Office. Scazzero says, "You choose the length of time for your Offices. The key, remember, is regular remembrance of God, not length. Your pausing to be with God can last anywhere from two minutes to twenty minutes to forty-five minutes. It is up to you."[38]

Solomon—the wisest man in the world at the time—wrote, "Above all things, guard your heart, for everything you do flows from it" (Proverbs 4:23). He believed everything concerning our life comes from our heart, so the best thing we can do is keep proper maintenance on our inner life. Attending to our inner heart, attitudes, and a listening ear is essential as we move out in missional ways and means. Good works will quickly become dead works if we are not drawing both our wisdom and strength from the power of the Holy Spirit on a frequent basis.

Developing Red Light, Green Light Habits

1. Are you more of a red light or a green light person? How difficult is it for you to hit the pause button and intentionally slow down?

2. Share your thoughts on the following quote from Henri Nouwen: "If we can detach ourselves from the idea of the usefulness of prayer and the results of prayer, we become free to 'waste' a precious hour with God in prayer." Do you currently practice the Daily Office or something similar? Explain.

3. Is the idea of observing a weekly Sabbath daunting to you? Does it seem unrealistic or achievable? How so? When thinking about taking the time to "do nothing" through Sabbath, does guilt factor into your thoughts?

4. What non-work activities do you enjoy? How often do you partake in these?

Seeing and Responding to God's Missional Work

1. At least four times this week, put aside ten to twenty minutes to simply listen to the voice of the Lord. Don't talk . . . just listen. Don't *do*, just *be*. Open yourself to just hear his voice. Be sure to find a place where you can be alone with no distractions.

2. Practice the Daily Office at least five days this week. If you do not have a book or outline that is helpful, either search for an online version, or you may want to purchase a version of Shane Claiborne's *Common Prayer*.

3. Plan and observe the Sabbath this week. Think through what you will need to prepare in advance in order to be able to rest and enjoy your Sabbath. It is not important what day of the week you make your Sabbath. Remember, the Sabbath is for you; you are not for it.

LESSON 8

WAKING UP FROM THE AMERICAN DREAM
God's Mission and Our Resources

IN THIS LESSON

Reflection on Lesson 7: Red Light, Green Light

Central Theme: The Kingdom of God and the American Dream

Biblical Reflection: Mark 4:18-19; 1 John 2:15-17; Acts 2:44-45; Matthew 6:24-34

Reading: Open Hearts, Open Hands

Reading Reflection: Heart Exam

Missional Action: Seeing and Responding to God's Missional Work

LESSON 7: *Red Light, Green Light*

1. Briefly share how you lived out the Missional Action from last week's lesson. How difficult was it? How did it change or influence the way you understand the fabric of your own life?

2. How did you see God at work in the midst of the Missional Action? What did you learn about where and how God is working?

3. What did you learn about yourself? What might you do differently next time?

4. What reflections do you have on the other stories that were told in your group?

The Kingdom of God and the American Dream

The Lord has provided a plan for a sustainable and vibrant society. It doesn't just *happen* though. God's plan as revealed to us through the Bible portrays a caring community of Jesus followers who are both sympathetic and sacrificial in their approach to their possessions and financial resources. If we hope to bear fruit for the kingdom of God, our eyes and hearts must be fixed on people and things beyond ourselves. Hard hearts and clinched fists go together. Our hearts must be open in order for our hands to be open.

1. Being completely honest, do you consider yourself to be overly consumeristic and individualistic in your current lifestyle? What areas of your lifestyle may need to change?

2. How should the concept of a caring community change the way a local church thinks and functions in a local setting? How should the concept of a caring community change the way you think and act on a daily basis?

Mark 4:18-19; 1 John 2:15-17; Acts 2:44-45; Matthew 6:24-34

1. *Read Mark 4:18-19.* In this passage Jesus says that three things—the cares of this world, the deceitfulness of riches, and the desires for other things—make the Word of God unfruitful in people's lives. How does this apply to you?

2. *Read 1 John 2:15-17.* In what ways have you been tempted by "love of the things of the world" as it relates to materialism and consumptive habits?

3. *Read Acts 2:44-45.* Other than giving money at church, how do you currently practice, or imagine you can participate in, sharing your resources?

4. *Read Matthew 6:24-34.* Reflecting on this passage, does worry affect you frequently in regard to your own daily needs?

Open Hearts, Open Hands

In spite of the recent economic recession, the United States remains the wealthiest nation in the world. We have more than enough to go around. Our biggest problem is not necessarily having enough. It is more likely that we are not sharing enough. As the body of Christ, the core values of the church embody the only viable answer to the issue of *enough*. However, the American Dream crashes against God's Dream for his kingdom to manifest on earth as it is in heaven. The values of God's kingdom clash with the values of this world on most every front. In one of the most familiar of Jesus' parables, we are confronted with the key to God's Word taking root in our lives, in order that we may bear fruit and bear taste of the kingdom.

> Still others, like seed sown among thorns, hear the word; but the worries of this life, the deceitfulness of wealth and the desires for other things come in and choke the word, making it unfruitful. (Mark 4:18-19)

The importance of this passage cannot be emphasized enough. Jesus says understanding this parable is the key to understanding all of his other parables (verse 13). It is the master key. Tens of thousands of sermons are preached every weekend across America. Millions of Bible-based books are sold every year. And a multitude of Christians read the Scriptures daily. But our culture remains unchanged. Our neighborhoods remain unchanged. Our cities remain unchanged. Why? How can this be? The truth is that we—the body of Christ—remain mostly unchanged. To be change agents we must be *changed* agents.

The "Isms" Thorns

If you have ever gotten yourself tangled up in a thorn bush, you know how aggravating and painful it can be. Thorn bushes in gardens or planting beds can literally wrap around plants and squeeze the very life from them, leaving them fruitless or eventually lifeless. Jesus says this is exactly what happens when our lives become wrapped up in the values and agenda of the present age. We can spend endless hours of Bible study and church activity with no appreciable fruit produced in our lives on account of our entanglement with worldly pursuits and concerns. The following "isms" effectively choke out not only our ability to live with mission, but also our imagination of what we could possibly do missionally.

One of the critical admissions for Christians is that consumerism has the propensity to shape and dictate our very identity. When our identification is one of consumer our true identity as citizens of the kingdom of God—strangers and aliens to earthly kingdoms—fades away. We can't even conceive of a kingdom life in terms of risk, time, finance, and energy. We just cannot get our heads around how we could possibly afford to be missional. The was exactly what the apostle John warned against:

> Don't love the world's ways. Don't love the world's goods. Love of the world squeezes out love for the Father. Practically everything that goes on in the world—wanting your own way, wanting everything for yourself, wanting to appear important—has nothing to do with the Father. It just isolates you from him. The world and all its wanting, wanting, wanting is on the way out—but whoever does what God wants is set for eternity. (1 John 2:15–17, TM)

Individualism, Consumerism, Materialism

The very essence of the church—the fragrance it emits to the watching world—lies in its living as an authentic community. In other words, the church doesn't *have* a social strategy; the church *is* the social strategy.[39] We have an unmatched opportunity to show the world the type of life that can never be achieved through social programs or governmental intervention. However, authentic biblical community can never be practiced alongside the American lifestyle of individualism. In my [Lance's] book with Alan Hirsch, *Right Here Right Now*, we wrote on this very issue:

> The plethora of New Testament Scripture that speaks of loving one another, sharing with others, and substantially caring for the poor make little headway into the imagination of most American Christians. These passages are simply not taken seriously. "I can't open my home up to that lady and her two toddlers. I know she has no place to live and I have a spare bedroom, but that's just not practical for me at this time in my life." Individualism and our desire for comfort and privacy chokes out the Word and our missional imagination along with it, nullifying our effectiveness as agents of the kingdom of God. Vincent Miller wrote about the shutting down of our imagination due to our fixation with the American Dream:[40]
>
>> Two generations ago, it was not uncommon for families to raise five or more children in small, two- or three-room houses. Our inability today to imagine how this was possible is a testament to the psychological skills we have lost. Now it is a common expectation that each child should have her or his own room. This social arrangement requires an enormous amount of resources and renders us less able to share our dwellings with others in hospitality. Social isolation and the burdens of maintaining a family in this system make it unlikely that other people's needs will ever present themselves. If and when we do encounter them, we are likely to be so preoccupied with the tasks of maintaining our immediate families that we will have little time and resources to offer. The geography of the single-family home makes it very likely that

we will care more about the feeding of our pets than about the millions of children who go to bed hungry around us.[41]

Even the most cursory reading of the book of Acts paints the picture of an open-hearted and open-handed Christian people who are fueled by an unrelenting, risk-it-all resolve. To become this type of people, we will have to make some serious choices that most likely will necessitate significant lifestyle changes. Just like an out-of-shape athlete, we must get our lives into missional shape. Many of us would love to run a marathon, but we love eating brownies more. By the same token, most Christians would love to make an impact in their communities, but they have not shaped their lives to be able to keep pace.[42]

Currently, the average American family lives in a home that is over three times the size of the average American house from the 1950s. This is despite the fact that family units are smaller now than they were fifty years ago. Another telltale sign of overt consumption in our culture is evidenced by the data regarding the self-storage business. It is a twenty-three billion dollar industry that rakes in more than the entire entertainment industry.

The Lord is pleased when we enjoy the fruit of our labor, but our appetites need to remain in check. God has carved out an economic design for the body of Christ that is full of life for us as well as others. In *How to Inherit the Earth*, Scott Bessenecker says:

> Those who are meek and who are submitted to the government of God will seek for his kingdom to come before all else, because they treasure this kingdom more than they treasure personal wealth. They are attentive to those who are weak and who are trampled underfoot by the powerful. They turn into great centrifuges of wealth, spinning their possessions out to those in need and stretching their arms out to those on the margins of society. This isn't trickle-down economics where a few at the top might slop some of what they have accumulated over the edge so that a drop or two trickles down to the masses at the bottom. Kingdom economics is pictured in the poor widow who was so insanely generous that she gave away the little she had to live on (Mark 12:41–44). In kingdom economics the followers of Jesus pool their resources and then dole them out to each one as they have need (Acts 4:32–34). Widows and orphans are cared for in their distress (James 1:27). Homes are open for the homeless and clothing is given away to those who need it (Matthew 25:35–36). The economic blueprint in God's kingdom works against personal increase and selfish accumulation and works toward distribution out to the extremities. Perhaps that's why Jesus said that it was impossible to serve both God and money; people can't submit to the desire for personal accumulation *and* submit to the desire for God at the same time.[43]

Speaking of money, Jesus said it is impossible for us to serve God and money simultaneously (Matthew 6:24). For our lives to genuinely be fruitful for the kingdom of God, most of us must change our habits and lifestyles. Junk food and easy chairs do not churn out Olympic champions. The church in the book of Acts (Acts 2:44-45) had a habit of selling possessions and property for the sake of giving the proceeds to help supply the needs of those in their community. A return to this mindset and tenderness of heart would certainly go a long way toward forming us as missional people.

Heart Exam

1. How "thorny" do you believe your life is right now?

2. In what ways do you believe consumerism and individualism have worked to shape your identity? Do labels and brand names matter to you?

3. In what ways could your faith community act as a "social strategy" for the needs of the needy among you?

4. In what ways do you feel like you can begin to prune away the thorns in your life?

Seeing and Responding to God's Missional Work

1. Set aside some time to look over your monthly budget. Examine whether or not you can find space to eliminate a current want in order to help with others' needs.

2. Choose a possession that you enjoy and care about. Give it away, or sell it on Ebay or Craigslist and give the proceeds away to someone in need.

3. Prayerfully consider your current living situation and vehicle ownership. These are most likely your two most expensive possessions. Are there changes you could make to position yourself to live a more active missional lifestyle?

LESSON

9

LIKE A GOOD NEIGHBOR

Knowing and Loving Your Neighborhood

IN THIS LESSON

Reflection on Lesson 8: Waking Up from the American Dream

Central Theme: Good News for My City

Biblical Reflection: Jeremiah 29:4-7; Matthew 5:14

Reading: Knowing and Loving Our Neighborhoods and Cities

Reading Reflection: My Role in the Welfare of My City

Missional Action: Seeing and Responding to God's Missional Work

LESSON 8: *Waking Up from the American Dream*

1. Briefly share how you lived out the Missional Action from last week's lesson. As you examined your budget, what stood out? Did you discover any space for deepening your participation in mission?

2. Was there anything you decided to sell (no need to disclose what it is) and pass along the proceeds?

3. What did you learn about yourself? What lifestyle changes have you settled on or are pondering for your missional future?

Good News for My City

Though circumstance or happenstance may appear to be what brought you to the place you live, as a Christ follower you can be assured that God has *sent* you on assignment as a participant in his mission to the world. Your locale is no accident. The people in your immediate neighborhood and surrounding community are the ones to whom the Lord has sent you and for whom he has raised up your church or faith community. As individuals and the collective body of Christ, we are called to seek the welfare of the very people we are living among.

1. The word *evangelical* comes from a root word meaning "good news." Do you consider yourself to be "good news" to most of the people you encounter throughout your day? How so?

2. Honestly speaking, do you consider your church or faith community to be—not just a speaker of—"good news" to the immediate neighborhood and surrounding city? How so?

3. How many neighbors on your street do you know by name? How many of them have been in your house?

4. Do you have any lonely, ill, or financially struggling neighbors that you are aware of? In what ways have you responded or do you feel that you could respond to those needs?

Jeremiah 29:4-7; Matthew 5:14

1. *Read Jeremiah 29:4-7.* In this passage God says to make a good life for ourselves but also to seek the welfare of the city he has sent us to. In what ways do you "seek" your city's welfare?

2. The Jeremiah passage also contains God's instructions to pray for the city he sends us to. Have you given this serious consideration before? How does the thought of beginning to pray for your neighborhood and city enliven you?

3. *Read Matthew 5:14.* In this verse Jesus says, "'You are the light of the world.'" Wow. Imagine that. Have you ever looked at yourself this way?

4. Are there currently any ways that your light is somewhat hidden under a basket? Does the idea of "good works" excite you or turn you off? How so?

Knowing and Loving Our Neighborhoods and Cities

READING

Most of us view our neighborhoods and cities as little more than the places where we live. We just hope for the best—for a safe, peaceful, crime free community with good schools, parks, employment opportunities, and arts and entertainment venues. But a missional person sees his or her neighborhood differently. A missional church views its community differently too.

A missional church is a fellowship made up of people who individually and collectively own the responsibility for the welfare of their particular community as a whole. If our hopes of becoming a missional church are to be realized, we must open our eyes to be missional people in the very places we live and frequent. This begins with the street we live on, which is our most immediate mission field. These pathways then stretch out to our towns, cities, and other corridors of residential and commercial activity.

Seeking the Best for My City

When we make conscious and committed decisions—on a daily basis—to seek the best for our neighborhoods and cities, life flourishes not only for us but also for those whose lives we touch. No matter how we reach out, even if it seems small to us, our cumulative actions become proportionately significant.

> This is what the Lord Almighty, the God of Israel, says to all those I carried into exile from Jerusalem to Babylon: "Build houses and settle down; plant gardens and eat what they produce. Marry and have sons and daughters; find wives for your sons and give your daughters in marriage, so that they too may have sons and daughters. Increase in number there; do not decrease. Also, seek the peace and prosperity of the city to which I have carried you into exile. Pray to the Lord for it, because if it prospers, you too will prosper." (Jeremiah 29:4-7)

Speaking of God's chosen people, Johannes Verkuyl said, "In choosing Israel as segment of all humanity, God never took his eye off the other nations; Israel was the *pars pro toto*, a minority called to serve the majority. God's election of Abraham and Israel concerns the whole world."[44]

As God's missionary people—the *sent* ones—it is incumbent upon us to constantly ask missionary questions. Some questions we should be asking regarding our neighborhoods are as follows: How would a missionary live on my street? What would he or she notice is missing here? Who are the poor, marginalized, and hurting in my neighborhood? In what ways would my neighborhood be different if God's kingdom came here as it is in heaven? What would *good news* be for my neighbors right here, right now?

My [Lance's] wife and I moved into a neighborhood and quickly learned of a man who lived in the house behind ours who most of our other neighbors considered crazy. His reclusive ways and unkempt yard and vehicle served to further distance any meaningful connection to those around him. I [Lance] began to pay little visits to him when I would see him outside—initiating a friendship. I discovered Jim[45] isn't crazy at all; he is just old. He used to be an early computer programmer and is actually quite brilliant. Knowing that Jim would have no one to share Thanksgiving and Christmas with, Jim now spends those days with my family. My wife and I could have easily given notice to one of the many Thanksgiving Day community meals or had a meal delivered to Jim. But the issue in this instance is not just the need of a meal. The relationship and "being with another" is just as, if not more, important.

Frank Laubach said, "The simple program of Christ for winning the whole world is to make each person he touches magnetic enough with love to draw others."[46] Jesus followers and faithful churches are cities on hills and lights in the midst of darkness. Even though people in the surrounding neighborhoods may or may not join churches, they will have no choice but to see these Christians and churches as essential components of the health and hope of their communities.

> "You are the light of the world. A town built on a hill cannot be hidden. Neither do people light a lamp and put it under a bowl. Instead they put it on its stand, and it gives light to everyone in the house. In the same way, let your light shine before others, that they may see your good deeds and glorify your Father in heaven." (Matthew 5:14-16)

A competent and resourced missionary can quickly react to needs while unintentionally communicating that solving the problem is more important than knowing the person with the problem. Agencies and government programs can do that. What these types of groups cannot do is something only another human can do—build meaningful relationships with the people in need. Urban missionary John Hayes writes,

> When missionaries start with the need, hoping they will one day get to know poor people personally, they are likely to be found ten years later, still addressing the need. They are welcome, even necessary, outsiders, but outsiders nonetheless. On the other hand, when mission workers start with poor people in empowering relationships, they are likely to get to the problems, together with the poor. The "work" typically starts slower and looks less impressive when relationship is prioritized before attention to the need, but it is more likely to be owned and reproduced by the poor themselves and, as a result, have a much longer lifespan.[47]

The church is *not* the kingdom of God. It is an instrument, or entity, within the kingdom. It is incumbent upon us, therefore, that we understand who we are and assume the role of *servant* for the kingdom of God. We are God's tangible expression of how he feels about the world. Most Christians are overwhelmed by what they believe to be their own lack of talents, giftings, or expertise to help others. The good news is that none of us must have all the answers, resources, or solutions. That is one of the things that makes community so colorful and creative.

In their excellent book on developing vibrant communities, Peter Block and John McKnight said, "We begin to see that the neighborhood is a treasure chest. By opening the chest and putting the gifts together in many different ways, we multiply the power of its riches."[48] Think of the street you live on. Consider the homes on either side of your house as they stretch in both directions. Think of the houses on the other side of the street. It would amaze us all if we really knew of the gifts and talents of the people living in those homes—not to mention the resources contained in their garages, sheds, and houses themselves. Block and McKnight write,

A competent community builds on the gifts of its people. It knows that a gift is not a gift until it is given. Before it is given, it is only a beautifully wrapped box in a drawer. It is a capacity held in exile. Gifts need to be named and exchanged, not only to create a competent community, but also to create a functioning family. This is a family that has discovered its capacity to produce for itself, together with a competent community, all that is required for a truly good life, a satisfying life. The tragedy of a dysfunctional family or neighborhood is that the potential gifts of its members are never given.[49]

The road to loving our neighborhoods and cities can begin as a treasure hunt. By prayerfully opening our eyes and ears, taking some risks to get to know others, and giving ourselves as servants, we can play a significant role in the future welfare of our cities.

My Role in the Welfare of My City

1. Up to the present, how seriously have you considered your street and neighborhood to be your mission field?

2. Peter Block and John McKnight said, "We begin to see that the neighborhood is a treasure chest . . ." Think of some of the talents and gifts your neighbors have. How could they use those gifts to help make the neighborhood whole? Share with the group.

3. What gifts, talents, and resources do you have that could contribute to the community treasure chest?

4. Are there any particular neighbors who you believe would join with you in a community "treasure" hunt?

Seeing and Responding to God's Missional Work

1. Each day this week, take some time to read the local newspaper and watch the evening news. Follow up by praying for the welfare of your city in light of what you know, asking God to bring his kingdom to bear upon those situations as well as the ones you don't know about.

2. Each day this week, pray for the people who live on your street. Specifically pray for them by name (if you know their names). Pray for their physical and spiritual well-being, as well as any trying situation they are facing that you are aware of.

3. Ask another neighbor to join with you in a neighborhood treasure hunt. Create a neighborhood "Asset and Skills Inventory" for neighbors to share items and services. You can create a Facebook page just for your street to post the treasures. Ideas can include:
   - Construction tools
   - Mechanic tools
   - Gardening tools
   - Offering a pickup for others to use when needing to haul small items locally
   - DVDs
   - Books
   - Tutoring
   - Tax preparation
   - Handyman type of household fixes
   - Fax machines and copiers
   - Music lessons

LESSON 10

MI CASA ES SU CASA

Facilitating Biblical Hospitality

LESSON 9: *Like a Good Neighbor*

1. Briefly share how you lived out the Missional Action from last week's lesson. How did it change or influence the way you see your neighborhood?

2. How did you see God at work in the midst of the Missional Action? What did you learn about where and how God is working?

3. What did you learn about yourself? What might you do differently next time?

4. What reflections do you have on the other stories that were told in your group

Welcoming the Stranger

The translation of the Greek word for *hospitality* is made up of two words—love and stranger. The word literally means "love of stranger." For this lesson the word *biblical* is used to help differentiate this specific form of hospitality from what usually comes to mind today when people hear the word "hospitality."

1. What is the first thought that comes to mind when you hear the word "hospitality?"

2. Does the definition of hospitality as "love of stranger" surprise you in any way? How would you define a stranger? Do strangers include more than those we simply do not know?

Matthew 25:31-46; Luke 14:12-14; Romans 12:13; Hebrews 13:2; 1 Peter 4:9

1. *Read Matthew 25:31-46.* Have there been times you have seen Jesus in "the least of these"? How might this passage change the way you understand hospitality?

2. *Read Luke 14:12-14.* How does the picture given in this passage differ from the contemporary image of hospitality?

3. *Read Romans 12:13, Hebrews 13:2, and 1 Peter 4:9.* In light of these passages, who is responsible for hospitality? What do you learn about hospitality from these passages? What does it mean to "practice" hospitality?

Recovering Biblical Hospitality

When most people hear the word "hospitality," they picture entertaining around meals, or inviting family and friends into their homes for a night of fun and games. Some may think of the hospitality industry, which includes hotels, restaurants, and cruise ships that work judiciously to create an atmosphere of friendliness and welcome. Or perhaps, church "hospitality teams" come to mind—teams that include greeters, ushers, and those who set up coffee and snacks for the Sunday morning gathering. In either case, "most understandings of hospitality have a minimal moral component—hospitality is a nice extra if we have the time or the resources, but we rarely view it as a spiritual obligation or as a dynamic expression of vibrant Christianity."[50] The fact is that over time the Christian community has lost touch with the amazing, transformative realities of true biblical hospitality.

Understanding Biblical Hospitality

The adjective *biblical* is used to help differentiate this particular form of hospitality from the conventional idea of entertaining. In the New Testament, the Greek word for hospitality is *philoxenia*, which is a combination of two words: love (*phileo*), and the word for stranger (*xenos*). It literally means "love of stranger."

In order to love the stranger and open our homes effectively, we need to expand our view of hospitality. Jesus commands us to extend the circle of hospitality beyond friends and relatives to include those in need:

> Then Jesus said to his host, "When you give a luncheon or dinner, do not invite your friends, your brothers or sisters, your relatives, or your rich neighbors; if you do, they may invite you back and so you will be repaid. But when you give a banquet, invite the poor, the crippled, the lame, the blind, and you will be blessed. Although they cannot repay you, you will be repaid at the resurrection of the righteous." (Luke 14:12-14)

Let's be clear. There is nothing wrong with sharing a meal with friends and family. In fact, shared meal times play an essential role in cultivating healthy family relationships and are an essential element of biblical community. But the practice of genuine, biblical hospitality is distinctive from the conventional view because it reaches out to undesired, neglected people who cannot reciprocate.

But strangers are not simply those we do not know. In the strict sense, strangers are those who are disconnected from basic relationships. Making space for hospitality is not only about creating physical environments that are welcoming to others, but it is also about the posture we take toward human relationships in general. It is about turning our lives toward those who are isolated. It is about listening well to those who rarely have a voice.

Hospitality is really about *inclusion*. It is about including others into our lives and our network of relationships. The opposite of inclusion is exclusion, which involves the actions of dismissal and rejection. The lack of welcome can be deeply hurtful. Do you remember a time in your life when you were excluded? Stop and think for a moment. How did being excluded from the lives and activities of others make you feel? Many people live a life of constant exclusion. Biblical hospitality, when rightly understood and pursued, has the power to break the bonds of exclusion and isolation.

When considering the idea of hospitality as more than welcoming the stranger into a physical place, it is worth noting that Jesus' words in Matthew 25:35, "'I was a stranger and you invited me in,'" do not refer to a particular physical location for hospitality. "Instead, the verse challenges us to examine our practices of welcome to strangers in every setting. Jesus' words are more closely associated with relationships than with location—I was a stranger and you received me into your group."[51]

Hospitality involves living life in a way that places a higher value on relationships and community than on consumption and productivity. Regrettably, this is counter to the prevailing philosophy of American culture. As a result, many are losing their souls.

Barriers to Hospitality

After a wonderful historical survey of the complex tradition of hospitality—including the words and activities of Jesus, the Apostle Paul, Martin Luther, and John Calvin—Christine Pohl writes:

> Even a superficial review of the first seventeen centuries of church history reveals the importance of hospitality to the spread and credibility of the gospel, to transcending national and ethic distinctions in the church, and to Christian care for the sick, strangers, and pilgrims. Granting that the practice was rarely as good as the rhetoric, still, we pause to wonder, if hospitality to strangers was such an important part of Christian faith and life, how did it virtually disappear?[52]

When did we lose the capacity to give and receive hospitality? Why has it virtually disappeared from the life of the church and from those who make up the church? The reasons are undoubtedly complex, but much of the move away from biblical hospitality can be seen in the changing view of the family. We have moved from family as an extended web of relationships that included aunts, uncles, grandparents, and friends to a very individualized, insulated, and in most cases, small "nuclear family unit."

The picture within most single-family homes today is one of both parents pursuing careers and working hard to take hold of the American Dream. The endless pursuit of a materialistic vision leads to a lack of margin in several areas of life. There is no money left over at the end of the month. No physical energy left over at the end of the week. No time for relationships left over at the end of the day. The lack of margin in our lives becomes an enormous barrier to opening our homes to others. Until we are willing to make hard decisions to create margins, there will be little time and space to welcome others into our lives.

However, perhaps the greatest barrier flowing out of our changing view of the family has to do with the perceived relationship between family and culture. Over the past few decades, the family has increasingly become a place to achieve safety and security from the "dangers" of secular society. As author Deb Hirsch points out, the home has become a fortress to protect the family from the evils of the world, rather than a place of welcome. She writes:

> This is "our" space, and those we may "invite" into that space are carefully chosen based on whether they will upset the delicate status quo, inconvenience us, or pose a threat to our perceived safety. In other words, visitors, especially strange ones, stress us out. And while this is in some sense culturally understandable, the negative result in terms of our

spirituality is that the family has effectively become a pernicious idol—a sphere where the commands of the *Shema* are no longer applied to the whole of life. Culture has once again trumped our social responsibility. In such a situation, missional hospitality is seen as a threat, not as an opportunity to extend the kingdom; so an idol (a sphere of life dissociated from the claims of God) is born.

It's not hard to see how this is absolutely disastrous from a missional perspective. Our families and our homes should be places where people can experience a foretaste of heaven, where the church is rightly viewed as a community of the redeemed from all walks of life (Revelation 21). Instead, our fears restrict us from letting go of the control and safety we have spent years cultivating.[53]

This bastion view of the family leads to a high level of skepticism and fear of strangers. We are fearful that the stranger is not like us. They may think differently. They may have different values. They may make us uncomfortable. Stemming from the fear of the unknown is a heightened desire for safety and security. We add extra locks on our doors, install security systems, and construct higher fences. On a recent trip, we were staying in a newly developed subdivision in a large suburb of Dallas. We were astonished by the ten-foot security fences surrounding every house in the neighborhood. Not only were the fences three to four feet above everyone's heads, but the pickets that formed the fences were overlapped to prevent *any* chance of someone seeing into a neighbor's life.

People are created as relational beings. God made us to be in a relationship with him, but also with each other. However, because most people have never experienced genuine hospitality, and do not know how to offer it to those around them, they continue to live lonely, isolated lives. As followers of Jesus, we must set the example and illustrate for others the transformative power of hospitality.

Pursuing Biblical Hospitality

When discussing the topic of hospitality from Romans 12:13, John Stott makes clear that a better rendering of the word "practice"—for the action we engage in regard to hospitality—would be the word "pursue." Christians were not to simply practice hospitality, but were instead to "aspire to" and "seek out" opportunities to welcome strangers into their homes and lives. To help make his point, Stott quotes the third-century Christian scholar Origen:

We are not just to receive the stranger when he comes to us, but actually to enquire after, and look carefully for, strangers, to pursue them and search them out everywhere, lest perchance somewhere they may sit in the streets or live without a roof over their heads.[54]

In most areas of life we fall short of God's best by what we *do*: adultery, lying, stealing, jealousy, anger, and so on. These are all examples of sins of "commission." Not so with hospitality. Here our error comes through what we *fail to do*.[55] It is a sin of "omission," not only because of the failure to lessen or alleviate the hurt of another—or as Origen states, that someone is forced to live on the street—but rather because of what is left undone in our *own* lives. Every time we turn away from another, our heart becomes a little bit colder. The doors to our homes close a little bit tighter. Our vision for what God is doing in the lives of others becomes a little less clear. In *Radi-*

cal Hospitality, the authors speak to the transformative power of hospitality in our lives when they state, "The real question is not how dangerous that stranger is. The real question is how dangerous will I become if I don't learn to be more open?"[56]

Biblical hospitality is an obligation. It is a spiritual discipline and a missional practice. It is the way of Jesus, but it is also a gift to others *and* ourselves. Both the blessings and difficulties of biblical hospitality are most deeply discovered only as it is pursued.

This has never been truer in my [Brad's] life as when my family made the decision (with the constant prodding of my wife, Mischele) to become a foster family. After seriously reflecting on the concept of hospitality and recognizing the insanity of maintaining a "home office" that was rarely used, we decided to convert the office back to a bedroom in order to be in a better position to welcome others into our home. The re-creation of space has opened the door (literally) to an abundance of blessings. It has created wonderful opportunities to not only welcome dozens of children into our home, but it has also provided multiple occasions to speak into the lives of parents who desperately need someone to walk alongside them. At the same time, it is only in the midst of pursuing biblical hospitality that we have discovered the troubles and difficulties of welcoming the stranger; the "strangers" as well as our own family have had to learn to maneuver a network of new relationships.

Pursuing hospitality, along with all the blessings and difficulties that come with it, is at times scary and radical. But it is worth the risk. Unless we find a way to open ourselves to others, *we* will be the ones to grow more isolated and frightened. "If we do not find and practice ways of hospitality we will grow increasingly hostile. Hospitality is the answer to hostility. Jesus said to love your neighbor; hospitality is how."[57]

Practical Ways to Live Out Hospitality:

- Invite people into your home. Invite neighbors for a meal, or perhaps dessert. Some people can more easily invite others over on the spur of the moment, but most people need to plan and prepare ahead. If that is you, then set a regular time each week or month to invite others into your home.

- Make a list of people in both your faith community and in your neighborhood who would be encouraged by your offer of hospitality. For those in your church, invite them to join you for lunch after a gathering. For those who live nearby, invite them to join you for lunch or a cook-out. Sometimes being outside is less threatening.

- Identify single parents in your neighborhood who need weekend childcare. Care for someone who is recovering from surgery. Provide short-term or long-term foster care. Talk with local pregnancy crisis centers about the use of your home for single mothers.

- Offer to host an existing small group from your church. Perhaps start a new group that meets in your home.

- Be a "home away from home" for college students or those serving in the military who are away from home.

- Hospitality isn't always about inviting people *in*. Provide hospitality at a local nursing home.

Opening Our Hearts and Homes

1. In what ways does an understanding of biblical hospitality change your regular practices?

2. Who are the strangers in your neighborhood? Who are the strangers in your community? What are some of the fears that you have toward them? How can you open your heart and home?

3. How did the reading challenge your view of family?

4. What first steps would you need to take to create space in your home (or church) to welcome children, teens, the elderly, students, and so on?

5. Besides welcoming people into our homes, in what other settings might we be more hospitable?

6. What might you have to give up in order to make room in your home and church for hospitality?

Seeing and Responding to God's Missional Work

1. Identify the "strangers" in your neighborhood. Make a list of those who are in need of hospitality.

2. List three things that need to change to allow you to make hospitality a way of life. Develop a plan to take steps toward being more hospitable toward strangers. Who is the first stranger you will welcome?

How might you respond to these same questions from the perspective of your church?

1. Who are the strangers who live around the place where your church gathers?

2. What needs to change in order to allow your church to be more hospitable?

LESSON

11

CHEERS
*Engaging Third
Places*

LESSON 10: *Mi Casa Es Su Casa*

1. Briefly share how you responded to the Missional Action from last week's lesson.
   What "strangers" did you identify in your neighborhood?

2. Share with the rest of the group your plan for becoming more hospitable. What areas of
   your life did you identify that need to change?

3. What other reflections have you had on Lesson 10?

4. What reflections do you have on the other stories that were told in your group?

The Importance of Public Space

Isolation is a word that describes the kind of lives many people are living today. More and more people are spending less and less time with others. There is less time given to civic participation, workplace connections, religious involvement, and neighborhood relationships than ever before. People are spending more time alone. One possible solution involves identifying and engaging third places in our communities. Third places are represented by public places of common ground where people enjoy the company of others.

1. What examples of increased isolation do you see or have you experienced in the lives of people? Are things really different than they were ten or twenty years ago?

2. What might be examples of third places in your community?

Luke: 10:1-12

In the book *Missional: Joining God in the Neighborhood,* Alan Roxburgh proposes that in Luke 10:1-12, the Gospel writer may be suggesting a new way to understand the church in relationship to public spaces.

Luke may be suggesting a radically different location for being the church when the Spirit is breaking our boundaries. What if one of the most important locations for the church isn't so much being centered *in here* as being located *out there*? What if an element of what God is saying to us in this passage is that the nature, meaning, role, and function of the church will be rediscovered only to the extent we learn to discern what God is up to in the interactions with people in public space and homes of our towns and village?[58]

1. Why did Jesus send out the seventy-two? Where were they to go?

2. How does the concept of hospitality play out in this passage?

3. What can we learn in interactions "out there" that we might not be able to discern "in here"?

4. What do you think of Roxburgh's suggestion that the church might be rediscovered only as it interacts in public spaces?

5. What questions do these passages raise for you?

Where Everybody Knows Your Name

In the late eighties and early nineties, one of the most popular shows on U.S. television was *Cheers*, which was set in a sports bar in the heart of Boston. One of the most popular scenes took place at the time in every episode when one particular "regular" would bust through the front door of the bar and everyone would shout his name in unison, "*Norm!*" The tagline for the show was, "Where everybody knows your name."

The environment within *Cheers* provides a perfect picture of a cultural phenomenon referred to as a "third place." Sociologist Ray Oldenburg coined the phrase third place in his 1989 book *The Great Good Place*. The extended subtitle of the book says it all: *Cafes, Coffee Shops, Community Centers, Beauty Parlors, General Stores, Bars, Hangouts, and How They Get You Through the Day.*

But what exactly is a third place? According to Oldenburg, the first place is our home and the people with whom we live. The second place is where we work and the place we spend the majority of our waking hours. A third place is a public setting that hosts regular, voluntary, and informal gatherings of people. It is a place to relax and have the opportunity to know and be known by others. It is a place people like to "hang out."

FIRST PLACE — HOME

SECOND PLACE — WORK

THIRD PLACE — COMMUNITY

Oldenburg identifies eight characteristics that third places share:

- *Neutral Ground.* People are free to come and go as they please. There are no time requirements or invitations needed. Much of our lives in first places and second places are structured, but not so in third places.

- *Act as a Leveler.* People from all walks of life gather in third places. There are no social or economic status barriers.

- *Conversation Is the Main Activity.* The talk is lively, stimulating, colorful, and engaging.

- *Accessible and Accommodating.* They tend to be conveniently located, often within walking distance of one's home.

- *There Are Regulars.* It is easy to recognize that many patrons are regulars at the establishment. But unlike other places, newcomers are welcomed into the group.

- *Low Profile.* As a physical structure, they are typically plain and unimpressive in appearance.

- *Mood Is Playful.* With food, drink, games, and conversation present, the mood is light and playful. The mood encourages people to stay longer and to come back repeatedly.

- *A Home Away from Home.* At their core they are places where people feel at home. They feel like they belong there, and typically have a sense of ownership.[59]

Why is it so important for Christ followers to understand the concept of third places? Because the vast majority of people in the U.S. are living isolated, relationally impoverished lives, and third places offer an opportunity for missionally minded people to do life in proximity to others.

In the book *Bowling Alone*, author Robert Putnam details the massive decline in social capital, which refers to the value of social relations and the networks of those relationships within a community. The title of the book comes from the fact that while the number of people who bowl has increased in the last twenty years, the number of people who bowl in leagues has actually decreased. When people bowl alone, they obviously do not participate in the social interaction and community discussions that occur in a league environment.

Putnam illustrates the declining trends in social capital in a number of other areas. He writes on the drop-off in civic participation in organizations like the PTA and Lion's Club. He then moves on to discuss the decrease in workplace connections, political involvement, religious participation, and simple informal relational connections. In one very telling example, he writes on the rise of card games in the post-World War II United States.

Although poker and gin rummy were popular, the biggest boom was in bridge, a four-handed game that had become extremely popular by the 1950s. By 1958, according to the most modest estimate, thirty-five million Americans—nearly one-third of all adults—were bridge players. Millions of Americans, both men and women, belonged to regular card clubs—in fact, one of the earliest scientific surveys of social involvement found that in 1961 nearly one in every five adults was a member of a regular foursome. In dorms and student unions of the 1960s and 1970s hundreds of thousands of college students spent millions of nights in seemingly endless games of bridge. The primary attraction of bridge and other card games was that they were highly social patterns. "Mixed doubles" clubs were, in that more gendered world, one of the most important sites for men and women to gather informally. The rules encouraged conversation about topics other than the game itself, since "table talk" about the state of play was generally frowned on.[60]

Let that sink in for a moment. Just a few decades ago, once a week, one-third of the families in the United States would spend the evening at the home of another family to play games and visit. Today, while there are substitutes for card games—everything from computer and video games to unlimited television choices—the reality is that we usually engage in them alone.

Oldenburg also speaks to the issue of isolation by specifically highlighting the disastrous design of suburban living.

> Most residential areas built since World War II have been designed to protect people from community rather than connect them to it. Virtually all means of meeting and getting to know one's neighbors have been eliminated. An electronically operated garage door out front and a privacy fence out back afford near-total protection from those who, in former days, would have been neighbors.[61]

The deterioration of social connections in our communities should drive us to action. As followers of Jesus we know that we were created as relational beings. We know that God designed us to be in a deep, abiding relationship with him. But we also understand that we were created to be in life-giving relationships with one another. The idea of millions of lonely people sitting at home, dying relationally from the lack of basic human connections should inspire us to bring about change. But what are we to do? Let us suggest three things in regards to third places.

Identify and Enter into Third Places

We must take the time to identify the third places in our setting. Where do people gather to spend time with others? Where are the coffee houses, cafes, pubs, and other hangouts? But in addition to the typical third places as described by Oldenburg, what are some "atypical" places where people congregate? Think of places such as libraries, parks, farmer's markets, workout centers, and so on. We may need to think outside the box when identifying where people gather. But once identified, we must seek ways to engage these places. As discussed in Lesson 2, this will involve embedding our lives incarnationally into third places, listening and learning where God is at work, and asking how we can participate in what God is doing.

Create Environments for Third Places to Flourish

This may mean that we take the huge step to actually open a coffee shop or bookstore in our neighborhood. Perhaps plant a community garden that creates opportunities for people to work together. Or maybe we create space in our own yard for neighborhood kids to play and spend time together. My [Brad's] family keeps an extra refrigerator in the garage, filled with juice boxes and popsicles. The refreshments provide a great "break area" between all kinds of games that regularly take place in the side yard of our property. Don't forget, as discussed in the last lesson on hospitality, that our homes may provide a sort of third place for our neighbors. Again, we need to be creative in the way we think about common space in our neighborhoods and how they may enhance relational connections.

Support and Defend Third Places

This may sound unusual, but in some cases we may need to become urban/suburban planning advocates. As already mentioned, we understand the importance of relationships for the health and vitality of our communities. Therefore, when there are plans proposed for such things as parks, sidewalks, walking paths, libraries, and anything else that would enhance the opportunity for a richer public life, we need to support such plans.

Our engagement with third places should first flow out of our desire to see those who are relationally disconnected drawn into life-giving relationships with others, and ultimately with the giver of life. But secondly, it should flow out of the recognition that as an increasing number of people are less interested in the activities of the church, it is we, as the missionary people of God, who have to engage others on common ground, or third places.

Identifying Third Places

1. Where do you recognize a sense of isolation or loneliness in your neighborhood? Do you yourself experience feelings of isolation from your neighbors? How does the gospel, the good news of the kingdom, address the issue of isolation?

2. Do you believe the sense of community in your neighborhood is increasing or decreasing? Why?

3. What are the easily identified third places in your neighborhood? Describe them.

4. Are there "atypical" third places that you can identify in your neighborhood? Describe them.

5. How might you go about entering into some of the third places that you mentioned?

6. How could you create a third place environment in your neighborhood?

7. What questions do you have about this lesson? What aspects of this lesson challenged or convicted you? Are there tensions you are experiencing with this lesson?

Seeing and Responding to God's Missional Work

1. This week discover at least three "typical" third places (as described by Oldenburg) in your community and three "atypical" third places. What would you have to do for each third place to become a daily or weekly rhythm in your life?

2. Pick at least one third place to enter into and spend at least one hour observing. Take note of conversations. What do you notice about the people? What is the vibe of the place? How does this third place bring life and vitality to the community? Where do you see or hear God at work in the conversations? How might you join him?

LESSON
12

TAKING IT TO THE STREETS
Starting Missional Communities

IN THIS LESSON

Reflection on Lesson 11: Cheers

Central Theme: Habits for Missional Communities

Biblical Reflection: Matthew 12:47–49; Hebrews 10:24-25; Matthew 5:14-16

Reading: Lighting Up the Darkness

Reading Reflection: Becoming a City on a Hill

Missional Action: Committing to Missional Community

LESSON 11: *Cheers*

1. Briefly share how you lived out the Missional Action from last week's lesson. Did you discover any space for deepening your participation in mission?

2. How has the idea of third places affected the way you view your neighborhood or community?

3. Is there a void of genuine third places in your neighborhood? Explain.

4. What lifestyle changes have you settled on or are you pondering for your missional future

Habits for Missional Communities

Though the philosophy and concepts of missional living may be something we understand cognitively, many people still struggle with actually living it out. This final lesson of *Missional Essentials* serves to give practical handles on what we have learned so far. By entering into some very simple yet significant habits—agreed upon by the collective group—your faith community can launch into fruitful and fun mission that is both measurable and self-perpetuating.

1. When you hear the phrase, "Let your light shine," what does that mean for your life? What habits or reminders may help aid you toward this end?

2. In what ways have the concepts from this study changed your day-to-day approach to life?

Matthew 12:47–49; Hebrews 10:24-25; Matthew 5:14-16

1. *Read Matthew 12:47-49.* What has your church experience been in relation to the idea of genuine family? How have you experienced the "family" of God?

2. *Read Hebrews 10:24-25.* This verse from Hebrews admonishes the members of Christian communities to assemble (meet) together and exhort one another by stirring up love and good works. In ways do you imagine this should happen?

3. Share your experience as part of a church or faith collective that purposely "stirred up" love and good works.

4. *Read Matthew 5:14-16.* In what ways do you perceive your faith community or church being a "city on a hill"?

Lighting Up the Darkness

It takes a community to reach a community. Communities of faith, sustained by a collective vision for reaching their host culture, are a vital means to the gospel going into the entire world. As we have learned from previous lessons, God doesn't have a mission for his church. He has a church for his mission. The late Francis Schaeffer said, "Our relationship with each other is the criterion the world uses to judge whether our message is truthful—Christian community is the final apologetic."[62] In other words, the best proof of the gospel of the kingdom of God is a people who are living out that gospel.

Early Christians embraced the new birth from the perspective of being born into a family. They understood that they were not born as orphans. Jesus interlaced the idea of family into his crafting of the early community of Christ followers. On one occasion when things were getting somewhat dicey for him, Jesus' mother and brothers came to intervene and bring him home. When they arrived outside the house he was in, someone told Jesus they were calling for him. In response he pointed to his band of disciples and said, "'Here are my mother and my brothers'" (Matthew 12:47–49). The early Christians understood they had passed from death to life, from the kingdom of darkness to the kingdom of God's dear Son, and they were not bringing their old life into his. That life was dead. They were not bringing their old sense of cultural entitlement into this new life. Those rights had passed away. This was a new society, a new culture, and a new community. To be in this new family meant you were no longer an *individual* but a *member*.[63]

Scholar Norman Kraus speaks to the missional attractiveness of the faithful community of believers:

In the New Testament, repentance means renouncing our old self-centered life and adopting the new lifestyle of agape (love) demonstrated by Jesus. This same community, which exists "by grace through faith," is also the community of witness . . . it has the character of a movement always remaining in and for the world. Jesus described it as a "city set on a hill," whose light beckons and guides the weary, lost traveler to the security and camaraderie of a civilized society. In the city there was safety from the marauders who took advantage of the darkness to rob and kill. In a friendly city foreigners could find protection and hospitality. Thus Jesus used the city as a symbol of the saving community, whose light shines in the gathering darkness, inviting the traveler to find salvation.[64]

Healthy families care for one another. They do not allow suffering to take place under their noses without breaking out all means to relieve and heal it. In the book of Acts, we see Christians who were "one another" people. They called each other *brother* and *sister* because they considered one another to be family. The early Christians' love for one another was a huge part of the collective *light* that was emitted throughout their cities and neighborhoods, causing Christianity to flourish.

Getting into a rhythm of mission is extremely important for missional communities. Committing to a common set of habits is one of the best ways to get started and to persist in mission. It is a way for each member to live out the apostolic commandment to "spur one another on toward love and good works" (Hebrews 10:24). In the most famous sermon ever preached, the Sermon on the Mount, Jesus told his followers,

> "You are the light of the world. A town built on a hill cannot be hidden. Neither do people light a lamp and put it under a bowl. Instead they put it on its stand, and it gives light to everyone in the house. In the same way, let your light shine before others, that they may see your good deeds and glorify your Father in heaven." (Matthew 5:14-16)

Below we have provided an acrostic derived from the word "light" to help you develop a set of habits and practices for your missional community.

Let's look at them:

Listen to the Holy Spirit
Commit to at least one hour per week of listening to the promptings of the Holy Spirit. Some members may choose to take a prayer walk or carve out a time of solitude and listening to God for an hour increment, once per week. Others may segment their hour into daily increments of say ten minutes per day for six days of the week. The point is to have a specific time of just listening in silence, not speaking or asking for anything, just letting the Lord speak to you.

Invite others to share a meal
Share at least three meals each week with others. Think in terms of people that are a part of your faith community and of those who, as far as you know, are not Christ followers. Share a meal with someone from each category. The third meal can be with someone from either category. The idea is that around the table, gospel things happen.

Give a blessing
Seek to to do three acts of blessing a week: one to a member of the Christian community, one to a non-Christian, and one from either category, as with the sharing of meals. Blessings can range from a simple email of encouragement to a gift of some sort, whatever is fitting. You are purposely seeking to be a blessing to your faith community and the broader world as well.

Hear from the Gospels
Commit to read from the Gospels each week in order to specifcally learn more about Jesus, his ways, and his means. The Gospels are always included in the weekly rhythm in order to constantly stay Jesus-centered. It is vital to read from other books of the Bible as part of your spiritual formation while always including a Gospel reading as part of your regular habit.

Take inventory of the day
This is a consistent reminder that we are God's *sent* people. As a faith community, we are a missional collective. We want to stay mindful of opportunities to engage in mission on

our day-to-day journey. To do this, keep a daily journal of how you have worked with Jesus during the day. Ask yourself how you responded to his promptings. Reflect on whether there were any missed opportunities or instances when you resisted Jesus during the day.

Grouping Around LIGHT

As your group meets together—weekly, twice per month, or monthly—the *L-I-G-H-T* habits serve another purpose. Missional community members have been living by them throughout their day-to-day lives, and now LIGHT becomes the outline for the sharing portion of your group time. Our suggestion is for groups to break apart into micro groups of three to four people and to go through each of the five letters, sharing personal observations, experiences, and learnings from the previous week(s).

Henri Nouwen said, "My whole life I have been complaining that my work was constantly interrupted, until I discovered that my interruptions were my work."[65] The Lord is *the* Creator and he lives in each of us. Therefore, there is no lack of creativity in any of us. We should ooze with imagination and ideas for missional living as believers and the community of faith. A sanctified imagination is a powerful missional tool because the fundamental job of the imagination in life is to produce out of the society we *have* to live in a vision of the society we *want* to live in. If we can just keep ourselves awake to the fact that we are God's good news people, life takes on renewed siginificance every day. Much of what we call mundane and routine can spark to life if we will allow our imaginations to come alive in a missional orientation.

Becoming a City on a Hill

1. On a scale of 1 to 5—with 1 being very weak and 5 being very strong—where do you feel that your current small group or church registers in regard to being a faithful family that is really "there" when members are in need? Explain and discuss as a group.

2. This question is not meant to illicit criticism but to improve the life of the group: In what ways could your group improve on being *family*?

3. On a scale of 1 to 5—with 1 being very weak and 5 being very strong—where do you feel that your current small group or church registers in regard to being a *city on a hill*? Explain and discuss as a group.

4. What gifts, talents, and resources do you have that could contribute to the community treasure chest?

Committing to Missional Community

1. Set a date for a common meal. If there is a group member who has never hosted a gathering, this is a great time for that person to open his or her home up for the *family*.

2. As a group commit to the L-I-G-H-T habits. When your group gathers, set aside some time to break off into micro groups to share your experience of walking in the "light." Come back together as a large group and share the highlights.

3. Agree to take the idea of "the family of God" up a notch. Ask every group member to share any tangible needs they currently have and then ask group members to respond with whatever means they have to do so.

4. Write down the name of each person in your group. Keep the list in a place you can see it everyday. Commit to pray for those members and the missional concerns, ideas, and upcoming events your group or church has.

1. Lesson 1: His Nature

1. Christopher J. H. Wright, *The Mission of God* (Downers Grove, IL: InterVarsity Press, 2006), 301.
2. John R. W. Stott, *Christian Mission in the Modern World* (Downers Grove, IL: InterVarsity Press, 1975), 23.
3. Alan Hirsch, *The Forgotten Ways* (Grand Rapids, MI: BrazosPress, 2006), 129.
4. George R. Hunsberger, *The Church Between Gospel and Culture* (Grand Rapids, MI: Eerdmans, 1996), 337.
5. Lesslie Newbigin, *Foolishness to the Greeks* (Grand Rapids, MI: Eerdmans, 1986), 124.
6. Ralph D. Winter and Bruce Koch, *Perspectives on the World Christian Movement* (Pasadena, CA: William Carey Library, 1999), 509-24.
7. Alan Hirsch and Lance Ford, *Right Here Right Now* (Grand Rapids, MI: Baker, 2011), 249.
8. *The Forgotten Ways*, 57.

Lesson 2: His Way

9. Alan Hirsch and Michael Frost, *The Shaping of Things to Come* (Peabody, MA: Hendrickson, 2003), 35.
10. *The Forgotten Ways*, 133.
11. Michael Frost, *Exiles* (Peabody, MA: Hendrickson, 2006), 54.
12. Ibid., 55.
13. Darrell Guder, *The Incarnation and the Church's Witness* (Eugene, OR: Wipf and Stock, 2004), 9.

Lesson 3: Joining His Purposes

14. Christopher J. H. Wright, *The Mission of God* (Downers Grove, IL: InterVarsity Press, 2006), 62.
15. Darrell L. Guder, *Missional Church* (Grand Rapids, MI: Eerdmans, 1998), 6.
16. *Right Here Right Now*, 67.
17. Alan Hirsch and Dave Ferguson, *On the Verge* (Grand Rapids, MI: Zondervan, 2011).

Lesson 4: Turning His Way

18. Johannes Baptist Metz, *The Emergent Church: The Future of Christianity in a Postbourgeois World* (New York: Crossroad, 1981), 42.
19. Henri J. M. Nouwen, *Making All Things New: An Invitation to the Spiritual Life* (San Francisco: Harper and Row, 1981), 42.
20. Craig Van Gelder, *The Essence of the Church: A Community Created by the Spirit* (Grand Rapids, MI: Baker, 2000), 82.

Lesson 5: Hear O' Church

21. *The Shaping of Things to Come*, 127.
22. Henri J. M. Nouwen, Michael J. Christensen, and Rebecca Laird, *Spiritual Direction: Wisdom for the Long Walk of Faith* (San Francisco: Harper San Francisco, 2006), 20.
23. *The Message* (Colorado Springs: NavPress, 2009).
24. *The Forgotten Ways*, 90.

Lesson 6: The Past Is Now

25. Walter Brueggemann, *Cadences of Home: Preaching Among Exiles* (Louisville: John Knox, 1997).
26. Stuart Murray, *Naked Anabaptist: The Bare Essentials of a Radical Faith* (Scottdale, PA: Herald Press, 2010), 52.

27. Ibid., 52.
28. Stuart Murray, *Post-Christendom: Church and Mission in a Strange New World* (Carlisle: Paternoster, 2004), 76.
29. *Exiles*, 5.
30. Adapted from Alan Roxburgh, *Crossing the Bridge: Church Leadership in a Time of Change* (Santa Margarita, CA: Percept Group, 2000), 25.
31. Christine Wicker, *The Fall of the Evangelical Nation: The Surprising Crisis Inside the Church* (New York: HarperOne, 2008), ix. See also David Olson, *The American Church in Crisis* (Grand Rapids, MI: Zondervan, 2008).

Lesson 7: Red Light, Green Light

32. Henri J. M. Nouwen, Michael J. Christensen, and Rebecca Laird, *Spiritual Formation: Following the Movements of the Spirit* (New York: HarperOne, 2010), 18.
33. Ibid., 19-20.
34. Sean Gladding, *The Story of God, The Story of Us: Getting Lost and Found in the Bible* (Downers Grove, IL: InterVarsity Press, 2010), 25.
35. Abraham Joshua Heschel, *The Sabbath: Its Meaning for Modern Man* (New York: Farrar, Straus and Young, 1951), 14.
36. Dan B. Allender, *Sabbath* (Nashville: Thomas Nelson, 2009), 42, electronic version.
37. Peter Scazzero, *Emotionally Healthy Spirituality: Unleash a Revolution in Your Life in Christ* (Nashville: Integrity, 2006), 157.
38. Ibid., 159-60.

Lesson 8: Waking up from the American Dream

39. *Right Here Right Now*, 56.
40. Ibid., 132-33.
41. Vincent Miller, *Consuming Religion* (New York: Continuum, 2005), 49.
42. *Right Here Right Now*, 138.
43. Scott Bessenecker, *How to Inherit the Earth* (Downers Grove, IL: InterVarsity, 2009), 72–73.

Lesson 9: Like a Good Neighbor

44. Johannes Verkuyl, *Contemporary Missiology: An Introduction* (Grand Rapids, MI: Eerdmans, 1975), 387-92.
45. Not his actual name
46. Frank Charles Laubach, *Man of Prayer: Selected Writings of a World Missionary* (Syracuse, NY: Laubach Literacy International, 1990), 217.
47. John Hayes, *Submerge: Living Deep in a Shallow World* (Ventura, CA: Regal Books, 2006), 181.
48. John McKnight and Peter Block, *The Abundant Community: Awakening the Power of Families and Neighborhoods* (San Francisco: Berrett-Koehler Publishers, 2010), 70.
49. Ibid.

Lesson 10: Mi Casa Es Su Casa

50. Christine Pohl, *Making Room: Rediscovering Hospitality as a Christian Tradition* (Grand Rapids, MI: Eerdmans, 1999), 6.
51. Ibid., 151.
52. Ibid., 6.

53. Alan and Deb Hirsch, *Untamed: Reactivating a Missional Form of Discipleship* (Grand Rapids, MI: Baker, 2010), 167.

54. John R. W. Stott, *Romans: God's Good News for the World*, (Downers Grove, IL: InterVarsity Press, 1995), 332.

55. Daniel Homan and Lonni Pratt, *Radical Hospitality: Benedict's Way of Love* (Brewster, MA: Paraclete Press, 2011), 41.

56. Ibid., 36.

57. Ibid., xxii.

Lesson 11: Engaging Third Places

58. Alan J. Roxburgh, *Missional: Joining God in the Neighborhood* (Grand Rapids, MI: Baker, 2011), 146.

59. Ray Oldenburg, *The Great Good Place: Cafes, Coffee Shops, Community Centers, Beauty Parlors, General Stores, Bars, Hangouts and How They Get You Through the Day* (New York: Paragon House, 1998), 22-42.

60. Robert D. Putnam, *Bowling Alone: The Collapse and Revival of American Community* (New York: Simon & Schuster, 2000), 103.

61. Ray Oldenburg, "Our Vanishing Third Places." *Planning Commissioners Journal* 25 (Winter 1996-97): 6.

Lesson 12: Taking It To the Streets

62. Randy Frazee, *The Connecting Church: Beyond Small Groups to Authentic Community* (Grand Rapids, MI: Zondervan, 2001), 85.

63. *Right Here, Right Now,* 186-87.

64. Norman Kraus, *The Community of the Spirit* (Scottsdale, PA: Herald Press, 1993), 170.

65. Henri Nouwen, *Reaching Out* (New York: Doubleday, 1975), 52.

NOTES

Printed in the USA
CPSIA information can be obtained
at www.ICGtesting.com
LVHW080221141123
763889LV00020B/358